Reading Thackeray

Reading Thackeray

MICHAEL LUND

WAYNE STATE UNIVERSITY PRESS   DETROIT   1988

Library of Congress Cataloging-in-Publication Data

Lund, Michael, 1945–
    Reading Thackeray.

    Bibliography: p.
    Includes index.
    1. Thackeray, William Makepeace, 1811–1863
—Criticism and interpretation.   I. Title.
PR5638.L8   1988   823'.8   88-1295
ISBN 0-8143-1987-4 (alk. paper)

"Beyond the Text of *Vanity Fair,*" *Studies in the Novel,* vol. 11
(Fall 1979), copyright © 1979 by North Texas State
University. Reprinted by permission.

For Anne

Contents

Preface

From Thackeray to Reading Thackeray

This book began in earnest on the train south to Virginia after the 1976 New York meeting of the Modern Language Association. At MLA I had heard a panel discussion of the question, "Do readers make meaning?" at a forum titled "The Reader of Literature: A New Perspective in Criticism and Teaching," featuring David Bleich, Stanley Fish, Normand Holland, Walter Ong, and Michael Riffaterre. As the Metroliner sped down the length of New Jersey, I rethought an essay I had written on *Vanity Fair*. As the focus shifted from an interest in the author's skills to a study of the effects these techniques might have on an audience, what had been conceived of as "a book on Thackeray" began a metamorphosis into this book about "reading Thackeray," a book not only about an author's skill but also about readers' responses.

The original essay on *Vanity Fair* had explored how, through the middle third of this great nineteenth-century novel, Amelia Sedley Osborne was pressured by circumstances to endorse her husband, George, as a good man, as a hero, and as a loyal husband. Refusing her brother Joseph Sedley's cowardly offer to retreat from Brussels in chapter 32 of the novel, Amelia imitated a nobility present in her companion Mrs. O'Dowd because any course other than waiting for her husband's orders was unacceptable in front of the wounded Ensign Stubble and others of her husband's regiment. But this public stance, adopted for the moment, became permanent when, on the next day, Amelia learned that George "way lying on his face, dead, with a bullet through his heart." Amelia's later foolish and sentimental adoration of her fallen husband can be traced to this crucial scene. That is, her fate in the rest of the novel is a product of the context that surrounded her at this key moment in her life. The dynamics of Thackeray's art in the scene, I had originally argued, were typical of his greatest writing, as we see that characters in Vanity Fair take on virtue more because of circumstances than because of their own beliefs or intentions and that even these apparent virtues are often later corrupted or falsified.

Thinking again about this scene, however, on the train leaving New York, I considered this text within the context of Thackeray's original audience. Just as I had considered Amelia's actions within the context of the actions of others, I now analyzed the readers' reaction within the context of their own situation outside the text of the novel. Not only, I realized, was Amelia pressured by the specific elements of this wartime scene, but so too were Thackeray's original readers affected by the mid-Victorian world of prosperity and stability that surrounded them. It would have been difficult for Victorian readers to view in unfavorable terms Amelia's defending her husband (and by extension, herself) from any suspicion of infidelity or cowardice; she is heroically rejecting Joseph's offer of retreat in order to stand by her British comrades facing the advance of the terrible French army. But in their admiration of Amelia from the armchair security of their position in the middle of the century, weren't Thackeray's readers also implicated in the psychology of Vanity Fair, admiring what is in the end a misplaced and undeserved loyalty? This immediately seemed true to me, and I recognized this as my first concrete example of how the critical method of reader response can change the "meaning" of a literary text. Thackeray's art did not simply reveal the vanity of Amelia; it demonstrated also the vanity of readers who, in admiring Amelia, gave in to a simplistic, sentimental view of human affairs. Later study of the rest of the text of *Vanity Fair* showed that the readers', more

10

than Amelia's, shallow and sentimental concept of heroism is the major object of attack in Thackeray's satire.

This initial discovery of the value of looking at literary texts from the perspective of the audience was augmented when I pursued my study of this key moment in Victorian fiction, because, like a great many nineteenth-century novels, *Vanity Fair* was first published in installments (twenty monthly parts in nineteen months). The serial form shaped audience reception in ways that traditional textual criticism had not always recognized. I realized specifically that the scene with Amelia, Mrs. O'Dowd, and Joseph Sedley came near the end of number 9 and was in fact the final image of Amelia the original serial readers took away from Thackeray that month (September 1847). Thus, the scene of a heroic, loyal wife asserting her husband's virtues remained in the Victorian audience's mind for a considerable time, at least until October 1847, and this period of waiting for news about the suffering Amelia deepened the audience's identification with such loyalty. The important temporal context that surrounds the text of *Vanity Fair* reinforces a thematic concern in Thackeray's fiction—what is the nature of heroism and what is the reader's relationship to it?

In revising my original essay, then, into "Beyond the Text of *Vanity Fair*," I had the first chapter in a book on the shape of reader response to Thackeray's fiction: there were parts of this classic Victorian novel that were not "in the text" but in the context of Victorian life which surrounded its first reading and which, under the name of *Vanity Fair*, became part of the world's consciousness thereafter. Amelia Sedley is not defined just by the words Thackeray penned in 1847–48 but also through the images perceived and developed by the Victorian audience who thought over, wondered about, and discussed among themselves this version of womanhood as she played out her life in the nineteen months of the novel's serial publication.

The Victorian "Thackeray" to whom we refer now is not, then, simply the biographical entity, 1812–64, nor the totality of his words, both fiction and nonfiction, which reached print in his lifetime; it is all those things plus the written and spoken commentary on his works by his contemporaries. The title of this book, *Reading Thackeray,* means, then, the creation of a part of Western culture by author and audience in the middle of the last century to which we refer when we use such terms as "Thackeray," "Thackeray's fiction," or "the works of Thackeray."

Another unit in the production of this "Thackeray," a culture's understanding of one author's work, comes with the bildungsroman *Pendennis* (November 1848–December 1850); but this new "Thackeray" also cannot be defined simply by the 768-page text (twenty-four monthly parts) of a Victorian master. The particularly long time of publication for this work—extended by Thackeray's illness in October, November, and December 1849—also influenced the original readers' understanding and interpretation of the printed text. Since the subject of this novel is a favorite Victorian one, the development of the individual from naive provincial youth to sophisticated successful urban citizen, the audience's time frame of reading added to the meaning of Thackeray's text by creating an analogue or parallel to the novel's form. As the protagonist grew up in the pages of Thackeray's novel, his audience was also developing in its own twenty-four months of living outside the story. These two instances of development, which I term in chapter 2 "Growing Up in Fiction and in Fact," tended to merge in 1848–50, extending and expanding the range of growth that is the novel's subject. Arthur Pendennis's growth is a matter of Thackeray's art and the Victorian reader's own progress toward greater maturity. The "form" of this particular bildungsroman includes not only the shape of a novel but also the time frame of readers' responses.

I also began to recognize, as I worked on this second unit of *Reading Thackeray,* the value of Victorian periodicals as sources of information about how serial readers actually responded to specific texts. The outpouring of affection and sympathy for Thackeray in his illness, which included excessive praise for his current novel, *Pendennis,* underscored how much the ongoing form of serial fiction meant to Victorians by the middle of the century, the year before the Great Exhibition. To find the regular creation of liter-

12

ature slowed or stopped in one of its major writers would have reminded readers of doubt about the country's and the individual's ability to go forward, to continue on a path of development and growth. Reviews of installments of Thackeray's novel written before it was completed (in December 1850) and the public statements, first in hopes of, later in thanks for, Thackeray's recovery from illness reveal the audience's intense desire to help carry the novel through to completion. Author and reader, novel and society, were insistent on growing up together. This audience contribution to the continuance of Thackeray's text through the period of his illness indicates that the entire literary experience of *Pendennis* is visible in other texts as well as Thackeray's. While no single periodical or reviewer can be said to represent a universal Victorian response to Thackeray's text, the vast and varied record of individual reactions is the best source scholars have of charting the audience's feelings which established cultural entities like *Pendennis*.

The third chapter in this project followed the same line of reasoning as the first two, into what I had begun to call "the space between numbers," the context of the audience's existence within which the individual serial installments of text found their meaning. The unusually large "gap" between *Pendennis*'s eleventh and twelfth parts, caused by Thackeray's being ill and unable to write, proved an especially good place to explore a more specific aspect of the audience's contribution to this novel's meaning. In those three months a contemporary debate about the nature of literary effort erupted in the Victorian periodical press, catching up such notable authors as Thackeray himself and his chief rival, Charles Dickens. The subject of this debate, which gives chapter 3 its title, "Novels, Writers, and Readers in 1850," was already a subject of Thackeray's ongoing novel; thus the debate outside his pages created a context within which his words were understood. Further, this context in turn influenced the text of another novel everyone was reading in the waning months of 1849, Dickens's *David Copperfield*. This work was, like *Pendennis,* appearing in monthly installments and also took up the question of what constituted work in an industrial society. Dickens's text, appearing after December 1849, contributed to the public consideration of work and literary production since David Copperfield, like Arthur Pendennis, became a writer; thus, it too added to the context in which Thackeray's novel was understood. Reading Thackeray, then, became an action that involved not only the general Victorian life which surrounded the reader; it also meant engaging specific creations of Dickens along with or even as parts of those of Thackeray.

While Thackeray's *Henry Esmond* followed *Pendennis* in 1852, reading this work, published in three volumes rather than serially, was for Victorians an experience considerably different from reading his first two major works of fiction. Both subject matter and publication format determined specific aspects of *Esmond*'s reception. The historical subject of an eighteenth-century political plot tended to distance much of the nineteenth-century world that had figured so strongly in the earlier fiction. Key concerns of the Victorian era were factors in understanding this novel, to be sure; yet those issues did not specifically add to an experience of this text in the ways they had in Thackeray's serial texts. In those cases, the space between numbers had provided extended opportunities for the audience's world to blend with the author's text, shaping or reinforcing key elements of the literary experience. "Building the House of Esmond" (chapter 4), however, was more a self-contained single event than an ongoing, regularly interrupted public or social activity in Thackeray's age.

If *Esmond* was a literary event that made less use of certain features of the readers' world than did *Vanity Fair* and *Pendennis,* his next major work of fiction, *The Newcomes* (October 1853–August 1855) may well be the novel that was most caught up by, and then itself carried forward by, an enthusiastic Victorian audience. Aware at this time of how much his satiric voice sometimes distanced him from the larger audiences of more popular writers like Dickens, Thackeray told what he termed an "old story" of the marriage of convenience, involving characters—Clive and Ethel Newcome and the Old Colonel—who became household favorites for the rest of the century. Capitalizing on an increasing sense of separation in the Victorian age's rapid development from its agricultural past into an industrial and urban present, Thackeray's fourth major novel made use of the separations inherent in the serial novel mode. Each month readers, characters, and author came together in intense relationships, only to part from each other for thirty days before a reunion. Reading this novel became itself an enactment of a fundamental event in Victorian life, parting; as readers added their own experience of weakening social and family ties to the story of the Newcome family, the Victorian audience itself helped create the "Old Stories in *The Newcomes*" (chapter 5). Particularly in its final double number (parts 23–24), *The Newcomes*'s depiction of the sadness of parting had become a powerful event in Victorian society, perhaps the most intense single moment in reading Thackeray.

While Thackeray was able to make use of the fact of separation in his readers' lives in *The Newcomes,* he was also able, in a later work, to employ the opposite force operating in his time—the promise of new beginnings that succeed each separation. In one of the paradoxes of the Victorian era, Thackeray's audience entertained intense contradictory convictions: that they were being torn apart by the forces of change, and that they were forever building a new society through that change. In his last, unfinished novel, *Denis Duval,* Thackeray drew on this latter belief, that amid the rapid dissolution of traditional ties Victorians could still initiate promising new relationships.

Linking Thackeray's unfinished novel with two other incomplete works by his contemporaries, Dickens's *The Mystery of Edwin Drood* (1870) and Trollope's *The Landleaguers* (1883), I argue in "Literary Pieces and Whole Audiences" (chapter 6) that Victorians engaged fragments differently than do twentieth-century readers and critics. This theoretical conclusion—that how the Victorians read was an extension of their beliefs—stands as the conclusion to this study.

Because they were accustomed to fragments (individual monthly or weekly installments) within the major publication format of their times, Victorians found the parts of *Duval, Drood,* and *The Landleaguers* significant literary works even though their full

15

stories would never appear. For Victorians, to read Thackeray's *Denis Duval,* then, meant to engage each of its parts in *Cornhill Magazine* within a context which assumed that fragments were naturally elements of an entire design, a design so accepted it need not actually be seen. That design, in fact, included a further assumption of wholeness in Victorian life, which made the future a logical and positive extension of the present. That I can link these three unfinished novels together in one analysis here derives from this assertion about the Victorian worldview. All pieces of the nineteenth-century universe, despite often intimidating evidence to the contrary, were ultimately believed to be on a path toward fulfillment difficult for us twentieth-century readers to recreate in our own troubled age. My effort to evaluate Thackeray's achievements in fiction follows the principle of returning to that path, to the points where his original readers stood as they engaged his works.

Of course, not all these elements of reading Thackeray appeared to me as a vision on the train leaving the Modern Language Association's convention in December 1976. Still, the change in critical perspective that occurred at that moment has altered the notion of "Thackeray" each time I took up another work in the canon, showing in new ways how the major works of his career affected his age. Not all of Thackeray's novels are discussed here; but *Vanity Fair, Pendennis, Henry Esmond,* and *The Newcomes* are often considered the four major works of his career. *Denis Duval* is included because of the special insights it offers into Thackeray's art, and also as a bridge, with Dickens's and Trollope's analogous works, to issues involving Victorian fiction in general. By attempting to put myself back in the place of Victorian readers, reading as they did, particularly within the monthly serial mode, I believe I have discovered additional mastery of technique by a major figure in the history of the novel. Making use of the context that surrounded and in many ways defined his audience, Thackeray engaged the consciousness of his times and altered its future. The journey we are on today is, to a degree worthy of study, the product of this direction.

Much of the material that follows has appeared as separate articles in journals over the past ten years. In fact, I might as well

16

argue that this book has already appeared in its proper format, as a serial. Gathering the separate pieces together here under one cover and attempting to reshape them toward a continuous argument, I nevertheless hope, like Thackeray publishing one of his novels in volume edition at the end of an installment run, to be addressing new audiences and old friends.

Acknowledgments

I wish to thank the many individuals who over the years have helped me in reading Thackeray, especially the following: Jerome Beaty, who first inspired my interest in Victorian fiction; Robert Colby, Norman Feltes, Guinivere Griest, Linda Hughes, Juliet McMaster, and Wilfred Stone, each of whom offered encouragement at key moments in my career; my colleagues at Longwood College, especially Martha Cook, Bill Frank, and Massie Stinson; and friends at nearby Hampden-Sydney College, Elizabeth Deis, Lowell Frye, and Mary Saunders. I also wish to thank the National Endowment for the Humanities Summer Seminars for College Teachers program, which enabled me to complete a draft of Chapter 3.

I am grateful to the following publications for allowing me to reprint, in altered forms, material which previously appeared as follows: "Beyond the Text of *Vanity Fair*," *Studies in the Novel*, vol. 11 (Fall 1979): 147–161; "Growing Up in Fiction and in Fact: Protagonist and Reader in Thackeray's *Pendennis*," *Dickens Studies Annual: Studies on Victorian Fiction*, vol. 12 (1983): 285–302; "Isabella and the House of Esmond," *South Atlantic Bulletin*, vol. 42 (January 1977): 25–38; "Literary Pieces and Whole Audiences: *Denis Duval, Edwin Drood*, and *The Landleaguers*," *Criticism*, vol. 28, (Winter 1986): 27–49; "Novels, Writers, and Readers in 1850," *Victorian Periodicals Review*, vol. 18 (Spring & Summer

1984): 15–28; "Reading Serially Published Novels: Old Stories in Thackeray's *The Newcomes*," *Philological Quarterly*, vol. 60 (Spring 1981): 205–223.

1
Beyond the Text of *Vanity Fair*

In his landmark study of the novel, *The Rhetoric of Fiction,* Wayne Booth noted that while every novel contains an implied reader (the author's assumed audience), modern criticism has often "ignored, lamented, or denied" (p. 89) the reader's importance in the literary experience. After 1970, however, a number of important works attempted to fill this gap. Wolfgang Iser in *The Implied Reader,* for instance, explored the reader's active role in specific texts, insisting that literature involves both a "prestructuring of the potential meaning by the text" and "the reader's actualization of this potential through the reading process" (p. xii). To talk of the text as a thing "out there," apart from any apprehension of it, then, is to falsify literary experience, as Walter Slatoff pointed out in his *With Respect to Readers:* "one cannot escape the fact that literary works are experienced by individual living readers and that it is this experience which makes them valuable" (p. 21). To some critics, the reader's effort is perhaps even more significant than the text: David Bleich's "subjective criticism" suggests that "it is the reader who determines whether a piece of writing is literature";[1] Norman Holland's psychoanalytical approach asserts that "a reader responds to a literary work by using it to re-create his characteristic psychological processes";[2] and Stanley Fish seeks "an analysis not of formal features, but of the developing responses of the reader in relation to the words as they succeed one another in time."[3]

Walter Slatoff has outlined the particular area of reader response that I wish here to pursue in detail, the "inevitable and valid
imaginative filling in and fleshing out which we perform as we
read" (p. 17). That is, though we frequently think and speak of a
fictional character, for instance, as being "fully realized," it can
never really be so—there would be no end to the detail that would
have to be included to satisfy the literal meaning of the term. What
actually happens when we read is that we are given by the text a
great number of key facts and features from which we infer other
necessary attributes and, thus, ultimately conceive of a complete
person, "fully realized." Slatoff goes on:

> When an author gives a character a name, he indicates he is creating a
> person and intends him to be perceived as such; our very use of the
> word "character" implies that what we experience is a person.
> This sort of filling in and rounding out is very different from the
> loose speculation, daydreaming, or psychologizing about the lives and
> motives of fictional characters that so irritates anyone who believes
> that reading must at least be guided and limited by the text. The
> phenomenon I am talking about is as unavoidable (so long as we read
> as men and not machines) as our assumption when we hear a voice or
> see a body that it belongs to a whole person. That this phenomenon
> does occur, that we must in some respects move beyond the text, of
> course makes it very difficult to determine just what constitutes a valid
> reading. Ignoring such responses reduces the difficulty, but also re-
> duces the value and relevance, of our work. (Pp. 17–18)

To put it another way, I will try to show here how some fictional
events deserve critical attention even though they do not actually
occur in the text. I wish to demonstrate how it is the reader who
"fully realizes" character—particularly Amelia Sedley—in *Vanity
Fair*.

Though his first major work, *Vanity Fair* (1847–48) remains
Thackeray's best known and most frequently analyzed novel. Many
critics have explored in detail the novel's style and its form, especially Thackeray's careful manipulation of the conventions that
governed popular sentimental, historic, and adventure fiction of the

day.[4] The form of the reader's response to this particular text, then, would seem to deserve a similar attention. In fact, Wolfgang Iser has already selected it as a pivotal work in his history of the "implied reader," terming it an "outstanding example" of a transitional state in the novel's history, where "the author-reader relationship is as different from the eighteenth-century 'dialogue' as it is from the twentieth-century demand that the reader find for himself the key to a many-sided puzzle" (pp. 102–3). Professor Iser echoes a number of Thackeray scholars in pointing out that, despite *Vanity Fair*'s unabashedly obtrusive narrator, much work is still left to the reader's imagination if the novel's actions and statements are to be appreciated in full.[5]

One aspect of the novel to which the reader is particularly invited to contribute is its plot or causality, which is often left open to the reader's interpretation. Plot in *Vanity Fair* is primarily the histories of two women: one, the shrewdly competent Rebecca Sharp, consistently exploits the conventions of high society to rise within it; the other, the compassionate but vulnerable Amelia Sedley, is exploited by Rebecca and others in their campaigns to achieve social prominence. Because the character and adventures of Becky have been so thoroughly discussed by others,[6] I will offer here only a brief summary of the reader's response to her career before considering in more detail the story of Amelia.

In both Becky and Amelia's stories Thackeray elicits the reader's involvement in the novel's causality by the careful use of the omniscient narrator convention. Although Thackeray's authorial voice repeatedly explains the novel's actions, his very thoroughness frequently leads to confusion rather than understanding.[7] In one early summary of the plot, for instance, the narrator gives much information about a rumored note of proposal to the young Rebecca Sharp but no clear picture of events and their cause-and-effect relationships:

> Thus the world began for these two young ladies. For Amelia it was quite a new, fresh, brilliant world, with all the bloom upon it. It was not quite a new one for Rebecca—(indeed, if the truth must be told

23

with respect to the Crisp affair, the tart-woman hinted to somebody, who took an affidavit of the fact to somebody else, that there was a great deal more than was made public regarding Mr. Crisp and Miss Sharp, and that his letter was *in answer* to another letter). But who can tell you the real truth of the matter? At all events, if Rebecca was not beginning the world, she was beginning it over again.[8]

The number of questions one might raise about this brief account suggests how such commentary, which at first appears to be helpful, only puzzles the reader. What did the Crisp letter actually say? In what ways did Becky solicit the letter? Who is this unidentified "tart-woman," or the equally unspecified "somebody" and "somebody else," and is any a reliable source? Is the narrator himself reliable in his parenthetical commentary, or does he actually care about the "real" truth of this case? What exactly is he suggesting in his ironic use of the terms "an affidavit of the fact"? Is Rebecca beginning or beginning again the world? Is this incident supposed to show that others are the cause of Rebecca's actions, or is it the other way around? Despite the wealth of commentary Thackeray provides, we will never know from the text. Although readers are guided through a number of possibilities by the narrator, their expectation of unequivocal or easy answers is in the end defeated, and they are left on their own to select some final version of the history of events. As Jack P. Rawlins has pointed out, the novel in this method turns to its true subject—the readers themselves—by frustrating their conventional expectations, calling attention to the inadequacies of certain modes of perception characteristic of the popular fiction readers of Thackeray's age, and our own.[9] Rawlins notes: "We read romantic novels with an easy moral absolutism and live according to a more pragmatic creed. By casting us as the characters of his novel, Thackeray asks us to account for the discrepancy" (p. 13).

While in some places too much commentary serves Thackeray's purpose of requiring his reader to establish certain aspects of Becky's story for himself, at other points the narrator's commentary is more pointed. The "famous little Becky Puppet," as Thackeray called her,[10] has consistently elicited admiration from the novel's readers for her artful successes in a world openly hostile to her. But, as Rawlins in particular has shown, each time we accede to Becky's morality by applauding her, the ever-present narrator reminds us that we have failed to judge properly the causes and effects of Becky's actions: "If we wish social success for her, we are discouraged by repeated reminders . . ." (p. 29). This is the same kind of literary experience Stanley Fish has argued is inspired by Satan in Milton's *Paradise Lost:*

> . . . in the early books, Satan's false heroism draws from the reader a response [admiration] that is immediately challenged by the epic voice, who at the same time challenges the concept of heroism in which the response is rooted. Subsequently, Satan's apparent heroism is discredited by covert allusions to other heroes in other epics, by his ignoble accommodation to the "family" he meets at the gates of Hell, by his later discoveries squatting at the ear of Eve in the form of a toad, and, most tellingly, by his own self-revelation in the extended soliloquy that opens Book IV.[11]

Similarly, in *Vanity Fair,* a novel with numerous allusions to Milton's epic, the readers' satisfaction at Rebecca's ability to ridicule the vanities of others in her climb toward acceptance in high society is gradually overcome by their growing awareness of the extent of her own unprincipled behavior: her eagerness to marry Joseph Sedley or Sir Pitt Crawley, her patronizing use of Rawdon and abuse of their son, her relationship with Lord Steyne, her later life on the Continent. Here again the novel's true subject becomes the reader, who is called upon to unravel carefully the fiction's causality, determining what character is responsible for which result. "What *had* happened? Was she guilty or not?" (p. 517), asks the narrator at one of the novel's most famous moments—Lord Steyne discovered alone with Rebecca by her husband Rawdon Crawley—and then, almost incredibly, does not answer. Here, and elsewhere in the novel, readers must decide for themselves: they must fill in, beyond the text of the omniscient but evasive narrator, the degree and nature of Becky's guilt, the extent of her culpability for the sufferings of others and of herself.

The readers' understanding of Becky, then, bound up in their developing responses to her continuing actions, becomes as important to the existence of a complete *Vanity Fair* as the actual presentation of those events in the text itself. Our relationship to Amelia, the other focal point in our response to the novel, has generally seemed less complex and, perhaps for that reason, has not been as thoroughly studied as our response to Rebecca's actions.[12] In this other major history of *Vanity Fair,* however, the reader also plays a vital role, actually helping to create the character and determine the fate of the central figure, Amelia Sedley.

Our earliest conception of Amelia's nature is a relatively simple one; we recognize her honest heart but regret her inability to understand, and thus protect herself from, those who are using her. We know from the start, for instance, that her love for George Osborne is pure, but idealized and sentimental: "He was her Europe; her emperor: her allied monarchs and august prince regent. He was her sun and moon . . ." (p. 112). Amelia, a "silly little thing" (p. 37) according to the narrator, is the innocent prey of individuals like George and institutions like Miss Pinkerton's which have formed her character. As long as she remains this passive victim, our sympathy for her continues at least to balance our exasperation at her weaknesses. When she abandons the passive role for an active one, however, our reaction to her subsequent fate is less sure. That moment occurs not in the text of *Vanity Fair* but outside it, in the readers' response, very near the middle point of their experience of the novel, at the end of the ninth number (of the twenty monthly parts in which the novel was originally published, from January 1847 through July 1848), at the end of chapter 32 (of 67). Joseph Sedley's invitation to his sister Amelia, to leave Brussels on the eve of Waterloo, is the occasion for a new relationship between reader and text, providing a fundamental impetus for the rest of our experience of *Vanity Fair.*

26

The transition in our conception of Amelia from passive victim to active participant in Vanity Fair is, in part, the product of one characteristic provided her by the text—her habit of refusing to admit unpleasant facts in her world. Although she begins even before her marriage to receive hints that her husband is not "one of the most gallant and brilliant men in the empire" (p. 119), she simply ignores the evidence (for reasons with which, by the way, Thackeray is not altogether unsympathetic):

> And she had misgivings and fears which she dared not acknowledge to herself, though she was always secretly brooding over them.
>
> Her heart tried to persist in asserting that George Osborne was worthy and faithful to her, though she knew otherwise. . . . She did not dare to own that the man she loved was her inferior; or to feel that she had given her heart away too soon. Given once, the pure bashful maiden was too modest, too tender, too trustful, too weak, too much woman to recall it. (P. 169)

Thus, although she "knows" in some vague sense about George's true character, she manages not to think of it, to continue the illusion of his greatness at all conscious moments. When her father is ruined, Amelia fears that the real George might not honor their engagement and so simply refuses to think about that future: "She lived in her past. . . . the business of her life, was—to watch the corpse of Love" (p. 172). When Dobbin engineers George's return to Amelia, she rescues her picture of him as "the greatest and best of men" (p. 187), suppressing any latent suspicions she had held. But it is not long before she is again pressured by events to recognize George's shortcomings. "They were only a week married, and here was George already suffering ennui, and eager for others' society" (p. 233). Worse, of course, is the fact that George's flirtation with Becky is not unsuspected: "A dim uneasy sentiment about Rebecca filled her mind already [on their honeymoon in Brighton]; and although they kissed each other most tenderly at parting, yet we know what jealousy is; and Mrs. Amelia possessed that among other virtues of her sex" (p. 239).

27

Though the truth about George's relationship with Rebecca becomes clear to everyone, the text fails to make explicit the degree of Amelia's own knowledge.[13] Does she really know, or is she continuing to make herself incapable of seeing?—a consistently evasive narrator refuses to say. Although he pointedly asks—"Did she own to herself how different the real man was from that superb young hero whom she had worshipped?" (p. 251)—Thackeray never presents any direct answer. The closest the text comes to showing Amelia's awareness is that the narrator suggests what she is not thinking. At the ball where George will later slip Rebecca a note proposing they run away together, Amelia witnesses at a distance her husband's attentions to her rival. Engaged in small talk with Dobbin (about man's impulse to gamble), Amelia "was thinking of something else. It was not the loss of the money [through George's gambling with Rawdon] that grieved her" (p. 278)—but further than such indirect statements the narrator will not go. At one point, though, the narrator explains his refusal to be more explicit in reporting Amelia's fears of losing George: "Have we a right to repeat or to overhear her prayers? These, brother, are secrets, and out of the domain of Vanity Fair, in which our story lies" (p. 251). As Rawlins observes, "Thackeray is explicit about the sides of life that do not fit into Vanity Fair, his famous veil is drawn over all scenes of honest emotion, grief, love, or religious faith . . ." (p. 26). Into such space thus deliberately left vacant by the narrator we readers step, here filling in Amelia's unspoken distress with our sympathetic apprehension of it. Again, Thackeray turns his novel to its truest subject, the reader, who this time must construct a realm of experience and knowledge more fulfilling to human desires than Vanity Fair. Amelia's suffering consciousness—torn between recognizing the truth and refusing to accept it—must be realized in the reader's response.

If by this method of omission Thackeray encourages the readers to round out for themselves Amelia's state of mind, serial publication accomplishes even more.[14] The last scene of the eighth number intensifies the dramatic portrayal of Amelia's consciousness, while still avoiding any explicit presentation of her thoughts. As George

28

prepares to march with the British army against Napoleon in the morning, Amelia lies in bed, at times in a slight sleep, at others more wakeful. When George comes to her bed, Amelia's "fair arms closed tenderly round his neck as he stooped down. 'I am awake, George,' the poor child said, with a sob fit to break the little heart that nestled so closely by his own. She was awake, poor soul, and to what? At that moment a bugle from the Place of Arms began sounding clearly, and was taken up through the town; and admidst the drums of the infantry, and the shrill pipes of the Scotch, the whole city awoke" (pp. 280–81; number 8 ends here).

In August 1847 the Victorian readers filled in for themselves the "what" of Amelia's thoughts—and had no occasion for their version of Amelia's prospects, or other future events, to be contradicted or confirmed until September. In modern editions of the novel, of course, we but turn the page and let the text continue to inform us, but for Thackeray's original audience how much idle time in thirty days might be turned to rounding out beyond the text the terms of Amelia's despair? How many blank pages from Tristram Shandy's text would be needed to represent in a spatial framework the temporal nature of the actual reading experience? Wolfgang Iser has explained in *The Act of Reading* how such breaks in a serial story inspire "a special kind of reading":

> The reader is forced by the pauses imposed on him to imagine more than he could have if his reading were continuous, and so, if the text of a serial makes a different impression from the text in book-form, this is principally because it introduces additional blanks, or alternatively accentuates existing blanks by means of a break until the next installment. . . . the reader is compelled to take a more active part by filling in these additional blanks.[15]

When *Vanity Fair*'s ninth number does appear, Thackeray continues, and even intensifies, the reader's creation of the character of Amelia Sedley.

Thackeray's technique throughout number 9 is to delay Amelia's confrontation with two dreadful truths: George's unfaithfulness and his death (the famous last sentence of the number is: "Darkness came down on the field and city: and Amelia was praying for George, who was lying on his face, dead, with a bullet through his heart" [p. 315]). How Amelia responds to these facts depends as much upon the reader as the text; as he proceeds through number 9, the reader creates, by anticipating, Amelia's sorrow. Left behind in Brussels when the army advances toward the front, Amelia is apparently able at first to subdue or repress any fears about George's loyalty by concentrating on the danger he is in. When she is paid a visit by Rebecca, however, her secret dread threatens to rush to the front of her consciousness:

> Rebecca's appearance struck Amelia with terror, and made her shrink back. It recalled her to the world and the remembrance of yesterday. In the overpowering fears about tomorrow she had forgotten Rebecca,—jealousy—everything except that her husband was gone and was in danger. Until this dauntless worldling came in and broke the spell, and lifted the latch, we too have forborne to enter into the sad chamber. How long had that poor girl been on her knees, what hours of speechless prayer and bitter prostration had she passed there! (P. 297)

Again, the narrator is evasive, demanding that the reader fill in for himself Amelia's "speechless" prayers: does she now desire deliverance from the truth, from her unfaithful husband, from potential widowhood, from her own illusions? Her behavior in this encounter with Rebecca reveals a mental tension very close to breakdown. She accuses her visitor: "'Are you come to fetch him from me?' she continued in a wilder tone. 'He was here, but he is gone now. There on that very sofa he sate. Don't touch it. We sate and talked there. I was on his knee, and my arms were round his neck, and we said, "Our Father"'" (p. 298). Amelia's account of her last moments with George is perhaps another product of a mind accustomed to reshaping reality, for the narrator's versions of that scene include no such details of a tender reconciliation (pp. 279–81, 290). As the scene with Becky continues, the reader recognizes that Amelia's thoughts are increasingly divorced from reality. A few moments after her outburst, "She had forgotten her anger, her jealousy, the very presence of her rival seemingly. For she walked silently and almost with a smile on her face, towards the bed, and began to smooth down George's pillow" (p. 299). When she is later found by Mrs. O'Dowd (the veteran campaigner, wife of the Major in George's regiment), Amelia is "almost crazy with grief" (p. 299) and later will seem in "hysteric insanity" (p. 309) as the cannon from Waterloo are heard in Brussels. This collapse of rational control increases the reader's participation in an approaching moment of dramatic choice for Amelia. From this unsettled state of mind she will eventually regain her composure by accepting as final certain assumptions about the nature of reality—and the reader will establish her new bent of consciousness before the text does.

Amelia's mind is made up when rumors that the French are about to invade the city inspire her brother Joseph to propose a retreat. With Amelia in this crucial scene are Mrs. O'Dowd, one of the few good characters in *Vanity Fair,* and Ensign Stubble, an idealistic youth who had been wounded and then returned to the city to be nursed by the two women:

> "I can't stand it any more, Emmy," [Joseph] said; "I won't stand it; and you must come with me. I have bought a horse for you—never mind at what price—and you must dress and come with me, and ride behind Isidor."
>
> "God forgive me, Mr. Sedley, but you are no better than a coward," Mrs. O'Dowd said, laying down the book.
>
> "I say come, Amelia," the civilian went on; "never mind what she says; why are we to stop here and be butchered by the Frenchmen?"
>
> "You forget the ——th, my boy," said the little Stubble, the wounded hero from his bed—"and—and you won't leave me, will you, Mrs. O'Dowd?"
>
> "No, my dear fellow," said she, going up and kissing the boy. "No harm shall come to you while I stand by. I don't budge till I get the word from Mick. A pretty figure I'd be, wouldn't I, stuck behind that chap on a pillion?"
>
> This image caused the young patient to burst out laughing in his bed, and even made Amelia smile. "I don't ask her," Jos shouted

31

out—"I don't ask that—that Irishwoman, but you, Amelia; once for all, will you come?"

"Without my husband, Joseph?" Amelia said, with a look of wonder, and gave her hand to the Major's wife. (Pp. 313–14)

In this carefully orchestrated scene, a number of characters respond to Joseph's proposal before Amelia does. Accustomed as they are to filling in Amelia's state of mind at this point in her history, the readers too, I suggest, think of likely answers before she ultimately delivers her own response here. That is, the readers create in themselves the state of mind that the character Amelia will later exhibit in the text.

At the beginning of the scene, Jos's allusion to the great price paid for his means of escape adds an additional unsavory element to his already cowardly offer, making everyone—including the reader—expect immediate refusal from Amelia, regardless of whatever evidence might actually support retreat. Victorian readers would have been aware, by the way, that the first reports from Waterloo were of a defeat for their own forces and would, thus, have felt the attraction of Joseph's offer. Mrs. O'Dowd, however, preempts a negative reply from Amelia, saying what, no doubt, Amelia and most readers are already thinking, that Mr. Sedley is acting like a coward at this time of his country's great need. Jos nevertheless repeats his offer, and this time "little Stubble," the "wounded hero," counters from his sickbed with an appeal to regimental loyalty and to woman's wartime role as nurse, encouraging again all of us who would not be thought cowards or traitors to anticipate a speedy denial from Amelia. But Mrs. O'Dowd substitutes her response for Amelia's a second time, presenting herself as a conspicuous example of the military wife's duty to await word from her husband before undertaking any action. Her momentary vision of herself accepting (a very fat) Joseph's proposal ("stuck behind that chap on a pillion") further ridicules that alternative, and the reader agrees to this assessment by thinking the same thoughts that lead to Amelia's "smile"—none of us would choose to appear in such a comic, humiliating pose. At Joseph's second repetition of his request, Amelia finally delivers her simple reply. After Jos's thrice-made cowardly offer, and the several heroic dismissals of it, Amelia's "Without my husband, Joseph?" becomes an eloquent final word indeed. But either at this point or sometime later in Amelia's history, the reader must realize that this action will dramatically affect the course of future events in *Vanity Fair*.

The sequence of exchanges and the gestures of the characters in this scene stimulate a chain of thought, which Amelia unconsciously follows, that makes her response not only a rejection of Joseph's proposal but also a denial of any suspicion of George's loyalty to his marriage. That is, the replies others substitute for hers encourage her to adopt a pose of noble heroism appropriate to them. The resulting unequivocalness of her own answer and her deliberate movement toward Mrs. O'Dowd equate George with the major—honorable wives are remaining loyal to honorable husbands. Amelia's response would probably have been similar had she spoken immediately to Joseph's offer, but the context of the entire scene has elevated her stance to a nobility that spills over to the object of her loyalty, George Osborne. Amelia's refusal of her brother's offer thus becomes a proud assertion of her marriage's sanctity at a critical moment in her life—she denies the suspicions that have haunted her, declares her husband's innocence, and accepts a version of reality that will lead to considerable suffering in her future.

This proud state of mind, however, actually exists at this point primarily in the readers' minds as they anticipate and participate in Amelia's rhetorical declaration.[16] The narrator does not now chronicle the thought process that culminates in her simple statement; and no further picture of Amelia or her thoughts appears in number 9 (except the momentary image, in the last sentence, of her praying while George lies dead on the battlefield). The starkly presented dramatic scene, however, with its artfully ordered dialogue, encourages the reader to take for Amelia a series of mental steps from confusion and doubt to heroic denial and conviction. When Amelia speaks at the end of this critical scene of the novel, her mind and the audience's are one, particularly since Thackeray's readers knew full well that Waterloo was in the end a victory for the British rather

33

than the rumored defeat. However, just as Rebecca's social triumphs elsewhere expose our complicity in the morality of Vanity Fair by eliciting our admiration, Amelia's history here ultimately reveals a weakness for sentimental and heroic attitudes.

Amelia's heroic pose of loyalty is intensified again in the Victorian readers' minds while they wait for the appearance of the next number of the novel; Amelia will, in fact, be frozen in this idealistic pose for a month. This fact of nineteenth-century reading experience is underscored by the familiar periodical practice of printing excerpts from the month's publication of fiction in the review sections of weekly newspapers. Thackeray refers to this practice in number 11 of the novel, entreating "the public newspapers which are in the habit of extracting portions of the various periodical works now published, *not* to reprint the following exact narrative and calculations [on "how to live well on nothing a-year"]—of which I ought, as the discoverer (and at some expense, too), to have the benefit" (p. 351). The *Illustrated London News* for 11 September 1847 prints the next to the last paragraph of *Vanity Fair's* number 9, describing the English army outside Brussels "receiving and repelling" the advancing French troops, in "Our Magazine Column for September" (p. 171). The excerpted passage begins with the phrase, "All day long, whilst the women were praying ten miles away"; it thus intensifies the Victorian audience's static image of heroic, suffering women (Amelia in particular) supporting their loyal men in battle. Thackeray's involvement of the reader in admiring a sentimental Amelia is extended beyond his text into the Victorian periodical text.

As Amelia thus awaits word of George's fate in 1815—thinking of him as a loyal husband and hero—so does the reader in September 1847 wait for word of Amelia's destiny, thinking of her as a loyal wife and heroine. As she ignores or represses any knowledge of George's unfaithfulness while she waits, so too does the reader, though probably to a lesser degree. And Thackeray prolongs the reader's conception of a courageous Amelia who displays unlimited faith in her husband even more by again keeping her in the background of events until the last chapter of number 10. The next reference to Amelia is, at this point in the reader's experience, a familiarly evasive one: the narrator wonders, "when Rebecca was flaunting at Paris, the gayest among the gay conquerors there . . . our Amelia, our dear wounded Amelia, ah! where was she?" (p. 327). When the narrator does finally give more than this kind of passing reference to Amelia or her situation, more than twelve months have passed in her life. Of what she has been thinking during that time we are as usual told little, though we may have thought much: "She has spent the first portion of that time [twelve months] in a sorrow so profound and pitiable, that we who have been watching and describing some of the emotions of that weak and tender heart, must draw back in the presence of the cruel grief under which it is bleeding" (p. 347). Once again her sorrow must be the reader's creation, existing between the lines of the text for many pages. We learn later that the birth of Amelia's son gives her life new meaning (the "child was her being" [p. 347]), but whatever understanding of her past and the child's father she has finally arrived at is clearer, more "fully realized," in the reader's mind than in the text.

The reader's conception of Amelia's state of mind created in the scene with Joseph and Mrs. O'Dowd, though, is eventually confirmed by the narrator and the novel's plot. In number 11 we are told that Amelia's doting on Georgy is related to an exalted image she has retained of her father: "She talked constantly to him about this dead father, and spoke of her love for George to the innocent and wondering child; much more than she ever had done to George himself, or to any confidante of her youth" (p. 377). And when the Reverend Mr. Binney offers to become Georgy's stepfather, her response is exactly what the reader has predicted: she "said that she never, never could think of any but—but the husband whom she had lost. . . . [On] the days of marriage and widowhood, she kept her room entirely, consecrating them (and we do not know how many hours of solitary night-thought, her little boy sleeping in his crib by her bedside) to the memory of that departed friend" (p. 379). And finally (in number 13) the narrator confirms precisely what the reader has already experienced: "All her husband's faults and foibles she had buried in the grave with him; she only remembered the lover, who had married her at all sacrifices; the noble husband so brave and beautiful, in whose arms she had hung on the morning when he had gone away to fight, and die gloriously for his king" (p. 445). During the six weeks or more of nervous collapse, when the doctors who attended her "feared for her life or for her brain" (p. 347), the noble stance she took defending her marriage to Joseph and the others had intensified to the point of unshakeable conviction she displays for so many years thereafter.

During her years of widowhood, in which Amelia worships her dead husband's memory, years described in the second half of *Vanity Fair*, the reader's original compassion for her as a helpless victim is lessened.[17] Although Dobbin has from the beginning represented a better man and a willing husband for her, it would be impossible to document the exact moment in Amelia's widowhood at which all readers would want her to drop the pose of noble loyalty to George Osborne they shared momentarily with her on the eve of Waterloo.[18] George's last appearance in the novel (before his death) had encouraged us to hope for his reform; gazing at the sleeping Amelia, her husband had thought: "Good God! how pure she was; how gentle, how tender, and how friendless! and he, how selfish, brutal, and black with crime! Heart-stained, and shamestricken, he stood at the bed's foot . . ." (p. 280). But while this apparent or potential change of heart might warrant a temporary suspension of the reader's judgment, it is hardly sufficient to make us accept him automatically as the untainted hero Amelia later claims him to be. Wherever in the second half of the novel the reader retreats from Amelia's apparently unquestioning faith, it is not until *Vanity Fair*'s conclusion (numbers 19–20) that Amelia herself openly abandons her illusions about George and is ready to recognize Dobbin's true worth. She accepts then the same moral Thackeray intends for his reader—that heroic stances are sometimes as vain and foolish as cowardly ones, that our dismissal of Joseph's offer of retreat is in its own way as artificial and rhetorical as "Waterloo" Sedley's later military posturing.

Amelia's coming to see the world more realistically is, of course, a major element in the novel's action. In the last chapter of the book, Rebecca Crawley shows Amelia the love letter written her by George and explains: "He wrote that to me—wanted me to run away with him—gave it me under your nose, the day before he was shot—and served him right!" (p. 658). The picture of history Amelia had enshrined in her heart is now at last abandoned; but what replaces it is, as usual, left up to the reader to determine:

> Who shall analyze [Amelia's] tears, and say whether they were sweet or bitter? Was she most grieved, because the idol of her life was tumbled down and shivered at her feet; or indignant that her love had been so despised; or glad because the barrier was removed which modesty had placed between her and a new, a real affection? "There is nothing to forbid me now," she thought. "I may love him [Dobbin] with all my heart now. Oh, I will, I will, if he will but let me, and forgive me." I believe it was this feeling rushed over all the others which agitated that gentle little bosom. (P. 658)

Amelia's education into the true character of men reaches at this point the fulfillment Thackeray foresaw much earlier in his composition of *Vanity Fair;* at work on number 7 he wrote his mother about the futures of his characters: "Amelia's [humility] is to come, when her scoundrel of a husband is well dead with a ball in his odious bowels; when she has had sufferings, a child, and a religion."[19] Although she still tends to idealize those she loves, Amelia does in the end admit one far-reaching mistake in her life.

The creative impulse for Amelia's fictional life, then, comes in large part from Thackeray's readers who helped to create and sustain her idealistic vision as they read about George's courtship and marriage of Amelia. As Amelia's response to this series of events was withheld from them, the readers filled in the details of her thoughts and feelings from the few actions and statements she did make. The idealistic faith in her husband's character the audience assumes for her proves a major causal force in the novel's history.

The readers' role in the literary event of Thackeray's *Vanity Fair,* then, is considerable, particularly as they become involved in the novel's plot or causality. In their response to one of the novel's two main characters, Becky Sharp, the readers find themselves called upon to purify their understanding of causality in Vanity Fair, to resist the temptation to approve her unprincipled exploitation of the corrupt social system to which they pay a certain measure of allegiance in real life. In their response to the other major figure in the fiction, Amelia Sedley, the readers' compassion is succeeded by a recognition that she has, to some degree, created her own misfortune. By glorifying her husband's memory Amelia cuts herself off from a potentially fulfulling emotional life in the present. The frame of mind that dictated such a course of action, as well as the suffering which followed from it, was conceived by the readers as they witnessed a series of events culminating in Joseph Sedley's proposal of retreat from Brussels on the eve of Waterloo. The impetus for Amelia's subsequent history in *Vanity Fair* was a rhetorically inspired, idealistic loyalty to an unworthy character shared by Amelia and, for a time, Thackeray's readers.

While the text of *Vanity Fair* (and, of course, many other nineteenth-century novels) has been studied extensively, the form of the reader's developing response, the "inevitable and valid filling in and fleshing out which we perform as we read" (to return to Slatoff's terms), has not received the critical attention it deserves. The careful use of the omniscient narrator convention (choosing sometimes not to tell) and of the temporal space between parts' publication has enabled Thackeray to engage the readers' creative ability in the filling in and rounding out of literary experience beyond the text.

In his second major novel, *Pendennis,* Thackeray also exploited the omniscient narrator convention and the time frame of serial publication, letting his audience add the force of their own forward-moving lives to his text. Framing this fiction in the established convention of the bildungsroman, Thackeray took advantage of the sheer length of publication—twenty-five months in this special case—to develop the character of the protagonist.

2
Growing Up in Fiction and in Fact

Although Thackeray's *Pendennis* (1848–50) had begun its appearance in serial form six months earlier, Dickens's *David Copperfield* (1849–50) figures as the first English bildungsroman in Jerome Buckley's standard study of the genre, *Season of Youth: The Bildungsroman from Dickens to Golding. Pendennis* clearly contains many of the elements in Buckley's definition of the genre: "childhood" (in sketches); the "conflict of generations" (Arthur's resistance to the direction of his mother, Helen Pendennis, and his uncle, Major Pendennis); "provinciality" (the world of Dr. Portman, the vicar of Fairoaks, and Mr. Smirke, his curate); the "larger society" (London's literary and social worlds); "self-education" (Arthur's literary apprenticeship); "alienation" (Pen as cynical critic of society); "ordeal by love" (his romances with the Fotheringay, Blanche Amory, and Laura Pendennis); and the "search for a vocation and a working philosophy" (the fundamental plot of the novel).[1] Buckley skips over Thackeray's novel, nonetheless, because of a serious weakness he sees in its central character; the protagonist Pendennis, Buckley claims, develops very little, "[i]nsofar as he 'develops' at all during a prolonged and protected adolescence. . . ."[2]

Recent developments in literary theory, however, are changing such fundamental concepts as "form" by which we have traditionally classified works of art and identifying new elements by which fiction creates and develops character. Susan R. Suleiman in her introduction to the anthology *The Reader in the Text: Essays on Audience and Interpretation* identifies "a preoccupation with audience and interpretation" as "central to contemporary American and Continental theory and criticism."[3] Suleiman sees this preoccupation as a "movement away from the formalist and New Critical emphasis on the autonomy of 'the text itself' toward a recognition (or a re-recognition) of the relevance of context, whether the latter be defined in terms of historical, cultural, ideological, or psychoanalytic categories."[4] Thus, the "form" in "the text itself" might be understood in relationship to its "context," that is, the "audience" that perceives it. Not Thackeray alone, but reading Thackeray remains the subject here.

The social and literary contexts in which Thackeray's second major novel appeared have, like those that surround *Vanity Fair*, been discussed in considerable detail in the classic work of Gordon Ray and in more recent studies by J. A. Sutherland, Edgar Harden, and Robert Colby.[5] *Pendennis* appeared at a time when the aftershocks of turbulence in Europe (the Revolution of 1848), continued religious debate inspired by such events as the Oxford Movement and new discoveries in science, rapidly altering literary standards in an expanding reading public, and the unsettling effects of relentless middle-class growth created an atmosphere of constant social and intellectual change. Thackeray as author is able to link his fictional events to this mood of the times by structuring the novel around contrasts between country (the old, stable life) and city (a new and changing society), between the traditional sacred philosophies (of Helen and Laura) and the modern worldly visions (of Blanche and Emily). That is, Thackeray surrounds the lives of his novel's characters with the furniture of the real Victorian world. Even under the pressure of monthly deadlines, Thackeray produced a sustained, detailed portrait, with commentary, of the full context of his nineteenth-century world.

While this cultural background has already been closely studied in many respects, the temporal framework that governs the reader's assimilation of Thackeray's text reveals additional ways in which the novelist utilized the literary resources of his era, particularly the serial format. The time involved in reading any work of fiction can be a tool used by the novelist to establish or extend certain features of his work. Thackeray's use of the reader's time, especially the months of serialization, suggests a consummate Victorian author realizing to the full the "form" of the bildungsroman, a major genre of his century.

The "audience" that read *Pendennis* in twenty-four monthly numbers from November 1849 to December 1850 was encouraged by the artist to add its own sense of passing time to the world of the novel. To define the "form" of this bildungsroman, then, within new and evolving critical systems, one must not only describe the protagonist's evolution in the text (as Buckley does); one must also attempt to measure the reader's development outside the text, as I shall try to do here.[6] In the new critical climate, as characters grow up in fiction, readers grow up in fact. Before considering in detail some of the ways in which Thackeray's reader grows up, I want to review first some more traditional ground concerning the ways in which his characters develop.

The central figure of the bildungsroman, Thackeray's protagonist, exists like all of his fictional creations within a comfortable Victorian view of character: he matures, but he does not change dramatically. As the author puts it in perhaps the most frequently cited passage of *Pendennis*,

We alter very little. When we talk of this man or that woman being no longer the same person whom we remember in youth, and remark (of course to deplore) changes in our friends, we don't, perhaps, calculate that circumstance only brings out the latent defect or quality, and does not create it. The selfish languor and indifference of to-day's possession is the consequence of the selfish ardour of yesterday's pursuit: the scorn and weariness which cries *vanitas vanitatum* is but the lassitude of the sick appetite palled with pleasure: the insolence of the successful *parvenu* is only the necessary continuance of the career of the needy struggler: our mental changes are like our grey hairs or our wrinkles— but the fulfilment of the plan of mortal growth and decay: that which is snow-white now was glossy black once; that which is sluggish obesity to-day was boisterous rosy health a few years back; that calm weariness, benevolent, resigned, and disappointed, was ambition, fierce and violent, but a few years since, and has only settled into submissive repose after many a battle and defeat.[7]

Thus, "it was the same Pendennis" (2:210) first introduced in number 1 of this history who appears before the reader here in number 19. That the "development of the mind of a worldly and selfish, but not ungenerous or unkind or truth-avoiding man" (2:236) is gradual, steady, and undramatic does not mean that Thackeray has failed to show the development he intended.

This fundamental philosophy of character also inspires a favorite point of view in Thackeray's fiction, the panoramic vision of history where one travels easily from present to past or future. Because characters "alter very little," their natures are not greatly dependent on time; the narrator can see the same identity at both ends of a decades-long continuum. In the following typical instance of time-telescoping vision in *Pendennis,* for example, the hero attends a "Dinner in the Row" during his emergence as a professional writer in London and is ignored by a prominent poetess:

Indeed, Miss Bunion having considered Mr. Pendennis for a minute, who gave himself rather grand airs, and who was attired in an extremely fashionable style, with his very best chains, shirt studs, and cambric fronts, was set down, and not without reason, as a prig by the poetess; who thought it was much better to attend to her dinner than to take any notice of him. She told him as much in after days with her usual candour. "I took you for one of the little Mayfair dandies," she said to Pen. "You looked as solemn as a little undertaker; and as I disliked, beyond measure, the odious creature who was on the other side of me, I thought it was best to eat my dinner and hold my tongue."

"And you did both very well, my dear Miss Bunion," Pen said with a laugh.

"Well, so I do, but I intend to talk to you the next time a great deal: for you are neither so solemn, nor so stupid, nor so pert as you look."

"Ah, Miss Bunion, how I pine for that 'next time' to come," Pen said with an air of comic gallantry:—But we must return to the day, and the dinner at Paternoster Row. (1:342)

The Pen of the future in this passage is, of course, "changed" from his pompous young self (not unfairly described as a "Mayfair dandy"); but Miss Bunion is also correct in asserting that much of the change is in how he "looks" to her (and how he will look that "next time"). Arthur has risen in the eyes of the fashionable world, and Miss Bunion is simply accepting that revaluation. Narrative leaps in time like the one in this passage are made in a world where people hold consistent if developing natures, changing as much in the ways they are perceived by others as in their private selves.

Thackeray's characteristic point of view and his belief in essentially stable character combine with a reluctance to depend exclusively on conventional concepts of plot in fiction to achieve the primary context within which the protagonist develops. Buckley points out that the typical bildungsroman hero undertakes a journey full of trials, "by parents, by money, by the city," that resemble tests faced by "the knights of old romances";[8] these trials constitute the plot of the bildungsroman. Pen's evolution from naive provincial youth to successful London author—highlighted by his changing relationships to parental figures (Helen and the Major), his loves (Emily Costigan, Blanche Amory, Laura), and his rivals (Foker, Pynsent, Warrington)—follows this pattern. But in Thackeray's case, it is not only this conventional plot that promotes the development of Pen's character but also the social conventions that create his identity as he moves through them. Thackeray says in a preface to the completed novel that the " 'exciting' plan" of a typical adventure story "was laid aside" (2:vi) in the actual composition because he knew his narrative gifts did not lie in describing action.[9] Thackeray's particular skill is the ability to chronicle the social poses and perceptions that define people. The first sentences of the novel set the pattern for his unique presentation of character development:

> One fine morning in the full London season, Major Arthur Pendennis came over from his lodgings, according to his custom, to breakfast at a certain Club in Pall Mall, of which he was a chief ornament. As he was one of the finest judges of wine in England, and a man of active, dominating, and inquiring spirit, he had been very properly chosen to be a member of the Committee of this Club, and indeed was almost the manager of the institution; and the stewards and waiters bowed before him as reverentially as to a Duke or a Field-Marshal.
>
> At a quarter past ten the Major invariably made his appearance in the best blacked boots in all London, with a checked morning cravat that never was rumpled until dinner time, a buff waistcoat which bore the crown of his sovereign on the buttons, and linen so spotless that Mr. Brummel himself asked the name of his laundress, and would probably have employed her had not misfortunes compelled that great man to fly the country. Pendennis's coat, his white gloves, his whiskers, his very cane, were perfect of their kind as specimens of the costume of a military man *en retraite*. At a distance, or seeing his back merely, you would have taken him to be not more than thirty years old: it was only by a nearer inspection that you saw the factitious nature of his rich brown hair, and that there were a few crow's-feet round about the somewhat faded eyes of his handsome mottled face. (1:1–2)

As the point of view of the passage shifts, providing "a nearer inspection," we become more aware of the Major's real identity beneath his artful appearance: he declines from a celebrated figure of London society—youthful, regal, military—to an old man in disguise—alone, balding, rumpled, retreating, perhaps even, like Brummel, shadowed by a hint of disgrace. When, near the end of the novel, we see the Major's "shaking hands, the wrinkled and quivering face, the old eyes weeping and winking" (2:320) as his schemes for Pen have failed, it will be not only a series of dramatic events that have produced this character, but also the multiple points of view, which have allowed us to see Pen's uncle fully in the end.

Similarly, the central character of Thackeray's bildungsroman, "who does not claim to be a hero, but only a man and a brother" (2:372), will not develop as dramatically as, say, David Copperfield, whose journey through life begins at an earlier point and is filled with many more exciting events that shape his character. In her fine article on Thackeray and time, Jean Sudrann accurately states that Pen's development in the novel is limited. In the end, she argues, "Arthur Pendennis simply drifts into domestic bliss."[10] However, as Sudrann goes on to say, Thackeray still makes "the reader himself experience the movement of time within the frame of the novel" by repeatedly turning to "the image of passing time"[11] in the narrative. His shifting perspective, presenting all the novel's characters in different lights and consistently remarking on the passage of time, insists that we recognize the characters' inevitable aging. Thackeray's narrative, however, insists that time passes not only in the protagonist's world but in the reader's world as well. It is to this process of the reader's growing up that I now wish to turn.

By a number of methods, Thackeray's narrative in *Pendennis* throws his reader back into the time frame of the real world, creating a second context within which Pen as protagonist develops. The real time involved in reading this novel, in its original serial form, was more than two years, a fact of the nineteenth-century literary experience seldom considered in measuring the impact of Victorian fiction. In twenty-five months, the serial reader can be said to have changed significantly. W. J. Harvey, one of the few critics to have considered the long novel as a special kind of fiction, has suggested that works that involve an extended reading time present unusual problems for literary analysis: "a massive novel enforces a prolonged and probably interrupted reading. To this extent the reader is himself much less a fixity and much more a variable. . . . [T]he writer *may* be able to manipulate and control to some extent this prolonged interaction of life and art."[12] After the famous passage about time, change, and character from *Pendennis,* which I cited earlier, Thackeray continues with an authorial intrusion that does "manipulate [the] interaction of life and art," drawing attention to the reader's existence in his own frame of reference:

> Lucky he who can bear his failure so generously, and give up his broken sword to Fate the Conqueror with a manly and humble heart! Are you not awestricken, you, friendly reader, who, taking the page up for a moment's light reading, lay it down, perchance, for a graver reflection,—to think how you, who have consummated your success or your disaster, may be holding marked station, or a hopeless and nameless place, in the crowds who have passed through how many struggles of defeat, success, crime, remorse, to yourself only known!—who may have loved and grown cold, wept and laughed again, how often!—to think how you are the same, *You,* whom in childhood you remember, before the voyage of life began? (2:210–11)

Both by the content of his commentary, and by the way it breaks into the narrative flow of Pen's story, Thackeray's direct address to the reader recalls him from the fictional world to the real world, making the reader recognize that time has passed in his own frame of reference even if it has seemed to pass rather uneventfully in Pendennis's world. Laying down this book he has been reading for five hundred pages (and for Thackeray's original audience, twenty-two months), the reader is made to confront the fact that he himself has grown older as he read.

In addition to such passages of authorial intrusion, another narrative technique in Thackeray, the extended flashback, also emphasizes the reader's time scheme and his existence in that frame. For instance, we begin this novel with Major Pendennis breakfasting, "according to his custom" (1:1), at his Pall Mall club, where he receives the urgent letter from Helen Pendennis announcing Pen's plan to marry Emily Costigan. Number 2 concludes with "the writing of those two letters which were laid on Major Pendennis's breakfast-table, in London, at the commencement of Prince Arthur's most veracious history" (1:64). This return to the reader's starting place reminds him of the time he has spent reading to fill in the background behind the writing of the two letters. Some sixty-three pages of text have interposed—narration of Pen's ancestry, early childhood, and acquaintance with the provincial acting troupe—and sixty days of events in the nineteenth-century serial reader's life. The Pen who awaits the Major has changed not in Thackeray's text but in the contexts of the reader's expanded knowledge and experience.

Thackeray's narrative method, which consistently refers to two time schemes, is also illustrated in the structure of chapter 8, entitled "In Which Pen Is Kept Waiting at the Door, While the Reader Is Informed Who Little Laura Is."[13] Pen awaits the interview with his uncle, which had been forecast in the letter Helen Pendennis wrote and the Major received in the first two numbers of the novel. Pen is called to the meeting by Laura: " 'Lead on, Laura,' Pen said, with a half fierce, half comic air—'Lead on, and say I wait upon my uncle.' But he was laughing in order to hide a great anxiety: and was screwing his courage inwardly to face the ordeal which he knew was now before him" (1:66–67). With Pen stopped at this moment of anxious anticipation, the narrator recounts a number of earlier happenings: histories of Laura's parentage, her father's relationship with Helen Pendennis, her early childhood at Fairoaks, and the Major's own love life. The narrator concludes his digression some ten pages after Pen was "kept waiting" at the door: "Thus it was that Laura Bell became Mrs. Pendennis's daughter" (1:76). When Pen is allowed to enter the room on the doorstep of which he was forced to pause, the reader's understanding of the situation has been developed considerably. The flashback moves the reader forward through time, while the protagonist is frozen in time. In a sense, Pen's character has been "developed" in the narrative, but not simply by the method of chronicling events as they occur. Pen's forward movement within the novel's time scheme resumes only at the end of this narrative interlude, as the Major effectively begins undermining his sentimental romance with the Fotheringay. The next eight chapters chronicle the coming apart of the engagement, of Arthur's growth as bildungsroman hero who learns (from the Major, from Bows, from Emily herself) more about the nature of his world and how to live intelligently in it.

In Thackeray's *Pendennis,* then, two kinds of time exist within which we mark the protagonist's growth: the time that measures the occurrence of events in the fictional world of the characters; and reading time, which measures the occurrence of events in the reader's world as he turns pages of the novel. While the first is, as in all novels of development, an important context for the protagonist's growing older, the second—reading time—is also significant, revealing Thackeray's particular skill at utilizing all aspects of his serial format. A passage in the novel's second installment reveals how the time that clocks events occurring in Thackeray's fictional world is often relatively unimportant. At this moment in the novel Pen is being called by the universal experience of youthful romantic love:

> Was Pen frightened at the summons? Not he. He did not know what was coming: it was all wild pleasure and delight as yet. And as, when three years previously, and on entering the fifth form at the Cistercians, his father had made him a present of a gold watch which the boy took from under his pillow and examined on the instant of waking: for ever rubbing and polishing it up in private and retiring into corners to listen to its ticking: so the young man exulted over his new delight; felt in his waistcoat pocket to see that it was safe; wound it up at nights, and at the very first moment of waking hugged it and looked at it.—By the way, that first watch of Pen's was a showy ill-manufactured piece: it never went well from the beginning, and was always getting out of order. And after putting it aside into a drawer and forgetting it for some time, he swapped it finally away for a more useful time-keeper. (1:39)

The gold watch does not serve to mark the time of fictional events for the reader; the different periods of Pen's life (when he got the watch, when it went bad, when he traded it, and when he fell in love) are instead blended together into one moment of reading. A later passage on clocks and time again suggests that the exact times of events in this fictional world are not terribly significant:

[Pendennis] did not come home [from Oxbridge] at Easter; but when he arrived for the long vacation, he brought more smart clothes; . . . And he had a new French watch and gold chain, in place of the big old chronometer, with its bunch of jingling seals, which had hung from the fob of John Pendennis, and by the second-hand of which the defunct doctor had felt many a patient's pulse in his time. It was but a few months back Pen had longed for this watch, which he thought the most splendid and august time-piece in the world; and just before he went to college, Helen had taken it out of her trinket-box (where it had remained unwound since the death of her husband) and given it to Pen with a solemn and appropriate little speech respecting his father's virtues and the proper use of time. This portly and valuable chronometer Pen now pronounced to be out of date, and, indeed, made some comparisons between it and a warming-pan, which Laura thought disrespectful, and he left the watch in a drawer, in the company of soiled primrose gloves, cravats which had gone out of favour, and of that other school watch which has once before been mentioned in this history. (1:172)

The many times referred to here—the years of Pen's father's medical practice, of his death, of Pen's early schooling, of his leaving for college, of the present—are so mixed in the complex sentence and paragraph construction that the reader recalls the earlier, similar passage about watches as much as he distinguishes the time scheme of fictional events. That is, clocks in *Pendennis* signal the passage of time in the reader's world as much as they mark events in Pen's life.

In this passage, we remember not only the various stages of the protagonist's development but also the stages of our own reading experience. Iser argues that such responses are crucial to grasping any literary text: "as we read, we react to what we ourselves have produced, and it is this mode of reaction that, in fact, enables us to experience the text as an actual event. We do not grasp it like an empirical object; nor do we comprehend it like a predicative fact; it owes its presence in our minds to our own reactions, and it is these that make us animate the meaning of the text as a reality."[14] In *Pendennis* we see Pen moving from his years at Grey Friars to his adventures at Oxbridge in the traditional growth of a bildungsroman hero; but we also are urged by this passage, which echoes the passage read 140 pages (or four months) earlier, to recognize our own forward movement in time as it is accentuated by our ongoing reading of the novel.

Thus, Thackeray uses two temporal frames of reference—time in the novel, and time outside the novel—to increase the sense of Pen's development as bildungsroman hero. When movement in one kind of time seems to stop in the fiction, action occurs in the other time scheme, so that, relativistically, there is always a sense of change and growth in the literary experience. If no clock is ticking to mark the passing of time in Pen's life, there is often a clock ticking in the reader's own time; and the reader, not always aware of the difference, registers a sense of time's passing and of a character's developing.

This narrative method, emphasizing the reader's movement through the pages of the novel as well as Pen's movement within the fictional world, is used extensively by an author who believes in the essential stability of character through time and in storytelling by flashback and other jumps in time. While the reader observes, the hero advances through time and experience; then the hero may be stopped at a particular moment of time while the reader advances through his reading experience. In order to encourage the reader's awareness of process in the fictional world, Thackeray even goes beyond these narrative techiques that draw attention to the passing of reading time. Specifically, he uses the reader's existence outside the reading moment—that is, the time between installments when the reader is not actually reading. As Iser points out, "the serial increases or enhances [blanks in the literary text] in order to stimulate extra curiosity" (p. 194).

Thackeray nearly always concludes his serial installments of *Pendennis* with the hero at some crucial moment in his history. In the thirty days before the next issue resumes the story, the reader, impressed by the final dramatic image of the number, extends Pen's fictional life in his own real time.[15] As Thackeray himself insists, "poetical figures live in our memory just as much as the real personages" (2:104). At the end of number 2, for instance, Dr. Portman

50

bursts out in amazement that surely Pen does not plan to marry the Fotheringay, inspiring a typical dramatic conclusion for the part:

> Pen put on his most princely air. "What else, Dr. Portman," he said, "do you suppose would be my desire?"
> Utterly foiled in his attack, and knocked down by this sudden lunge of Pen's, the Doctor could only gasp out, "Mrs. Pendennis, ma'am, send for the Major."
> "Send for the Major? with all my heart," said Arthur Prince of Pendennis and Grand Duke of Fairoaks, with a most superb wave of the hand. And the colloquy terminated by the writing of those two letters which were laid on Major Pendennis's breakfast-table, in London, at the commencement of Prince Arthur's most veracious history. (1:64).

Arthur maintains this majestic pose for the original parts reader much longer than he does for the modern single-volume reader. The major begins the erosion of Pen's sentimental, grand gesture immediately in the next chapter: "Our acquaintance, Major Arthur Pendennis, arrived in due time at Fairoaks . . ." (1:65). While the modern reader contemplates Pen's bold statement for only a second, the Victorian serial reader witnesses Pen's heroics for a precise length of (real) time—from December 1848 to January 1849. The process of Pen's development as bildungsroman hero is significantly expanded and deepened in Thackeray's original format.

This tactic of making Pen's final appearance in a number one of his sentimental, pompous, or egotistical moments dominates the installment structure of *Pendennis*, figuring in sixteen of the twenty-two parts (excluding the final double number).[16] Pen is seen rejecting the unexciting company of Dr. Portman (end of number 1); bravely awaiting the outcome of Costigan's interview with the Major (number 3); eagerly departing for Oxbridge (number 5); romantically inspired by Blanche Amory (number 7); dining ostentatiously in London (number 11); envisioning himself as a new literary star (number 10); appearing as the aloof, cynical, worldly lover (numbers 12, 19, 20, 21); proudly aware of his first success as a novelist (number 13); taking the stance of profound philosopher (number 14); playing the role of noble patron of the lower classes, particularly Fanny Bolton (number 15); looking self-consciously repentant (number 17); and rising to nobility as squire of Fairoaks (number 18). After each of these appearances at or near the conclusion of a monthly installment, the reader takes over the imaging of Pendennis, the young protagonist with the exaggerated sense of himself, doomed for yet another fall. That fall, or the undermining of the hero's pompous stance, starts again with the resumption of text, in the next issue of serial publication. In the meantime, Thackeray has used the real time of the reader's existence to lengthen the process of the protagonist's growth.

Certain aspects of Pendennis's life are specifically given additional existence in the readers' world as they wait between numbers. When Pen's mother discovers Fanny Bolton attending her sick son in his London chambers (at the end of number 16), for instance, the reader is given thirty days to speculate about the nature and extent of the young protagonist's mistakes. Of course, his actions are hardly as lamentable as Helen believes (or the reader might have suspected), but Thackeray's use of the serial format intensifies his character's life and our reactions to it. Thackeray allows his protagonist to fall considerably in the world's eyes during that month-long delay in the resolution of the plot, and then Pen turns out to be innocent enough to serve still as a novel's hero. It is almost as if Pendennis receives all the benefits of guilt (in the intensity of the reader's reaction) but then ends up innocent of all charges.[17] Pen's recovery, both from sickness and from infatuation (in number 17), is also not as sudden as it might now seem to single-volume readers. "Our duty now is to record a fact concerning Pendennis," explains the narrator, "which, however shameful and disgraceful, when told regarding the chief personage and Godfather of a novel, must, nevertheless, be made known to the public who reads his veritable memoirs. Having gone to bed ill with fever, and suffering to a certain degree under the passion of love . . . when he rallied up from his bodily ailment, his mental malady had likewise quitted

him, and he was no more in love with Fanny Bolton than you or
I . . ." (2:139). When we recall *Pendennis*'s original format, we
realize that Pen has not been ill for a mere ten pages, but in the
reader's mind, for at least thirty days. Thus, major events in the
protagonist's life—infatuation, sickness, and recovery—are intensified and lengthened by Thackeray's use of the serial form, by his
use of time outside of his fiction as well as time within his fiction.

Thackeray similarly uses breaks in his serial publication to inten-
sify the hero's growing attachment to Blanche Amory near the end
of the novel, and to appear to reduce the chances of his marrying
Laura, the clear heroine of the story. That is, the final resolution of
Pen's fate and the entire novel are developed in the reader's time as
well as in the time of the novel. At the end of number 20, Thackeray's narrator seems to insist that marriage to Blanche is all that
awaits his jaded hero whose youthful passions, we are led to believe,
are forever behind him:

> Ah! What answer is given to those [tears] in the eyes of a young
> woman? What is the method employed for drying them? What took
> place? O ringdoves and roses, O dews and wildflowers, O waving
> greenwoods and balmy airs of summer! Here were two battered Lon-
> don rakes, taking themselves in for a moment, and fancying that they
> were in love with each other, like Phillis and Corydon!
>
> When one thinks of country houses and country walks, one won-
> ders that any man is left unmarried. (2:256; number 20 ends here)

When Pen later announces to his uncle that he plans to marry
Blanche even though he does not love her and she will have no
fortune, the reader is again urged to conclude that no escape is
likely:

> Arthur took his [the Major's] hand, which the old man left to him; it
> was quite passive and clammy. He looked much oldened; and it
> seemed as if the contest and defeat had quite broken him.
>
> On the next day he kept his bed, and refused to see his nephew.
> (2:320; number 22 ends here)

Since this is the end of the next-to-last installment (the last being a traditional double number, parts 23 and 24), the reader is encouraged by this memorable final scene to anticipate an inevitable, sad conclusion to the protagonist's romantic life. Pen's self-sacrificing decision to accept a fate created by his own mistakes is given additional force in the literary experience; in the reader's time between numbers 20 and 21 and between numbers 22 and 23–24, Thackeray's audience expands these images of the protagonist rejecting his worldly uncle's offer and maturing in his own vision of the world and his place in it. In the space between numbers the reader adds to the development of the protagonist in Thackeray's bildungsroman.[18]

One of the spaces between numbers for this particular novel is longer than the others. In the course of publication, Thackeray became ill and the issue of number 12 was delayed from October 1849 to January 1850. During this three-month interruption in the original reading of Thackeray's bildungsroman, the reader expanded elements of the novel even more than usual, and one key feature of all installment literary experience was underscored—the reader's inevitable affection for the characters.[19] Number 11 of *Pendennis* ends with Pen, the literary critic, suffering the first unfavorable review of his poems at the hands of a competitor: Mr. Bludyer, the reviewer, "had a certain notoriety in his profession, and reputation for savage humor. He smashed and trampled down the poor spring flowers [Pen's poems] with no more mercy than a bull would have on a parterre; and having cut up the volume to his heart's content, went and sold it at a bookstall, and purchased a pint of brandy with the proceeds of the volume" (1:352). This unflattering picture of the literary profession at the conclusion of the number, and others in the same issue, led to an extended debate in the press among John Forster, Thackeray, and others about the integrity of Victorian letters.[20] Part of the reason for the intensity of the debate, as I explain in chapter 3, may have been the extra time number 11 of *Pendennis* stayed on the public's mind before it was succeeded by number 12—three times as long as usual. The extra long time between installments also added to the audience's involvement with the career of Arthur Pendennis, the protagonist of the novel.

Although Thackeray himself was unable in those three months to further the development of the central character in his bildungs-roman, his original reader lived with the novel's protagonist three months longer. When number 12 of *Pendennis* did appear, it was warmly received by its readers, perhaps more warmly than it merited.[21] One reader's response to the reappearance of the lost fictional family of *Pendennis* is typical of the uncritical reception Thackeray was allowed after his sickness and suggests the involvement his audience had with his characters:

> There were many thousands of readers who, when it was announced in the public prints, that owing to the serious indisposition of the author, the periodical issue of *Pendennis* was temporarily suspended, took the matter to heart as though some dear friend and cherished companion had been suddenly smitten like a child at play, and carried from the bright, cheerful, outer atmosphere to the darkness and stillness of the sick-chamber. He was lost to us for a while, and we missed him. Many, it is true, had freely exercised the "glorious privilege" of grumbling, and had complained, with critical regularity, once a month, that *Pendennis* was a "falling-off—not equal to *Vanity Fair;*" but they did not like to go without it for all that, and pushed eager questions into every quarter about the chance of its reappearance. And when it reappeared, after a painful interval of some months, grumblers and admirers alike rejoiced.[22]

Despite reservations about the quality of the novel, and even the attractiveness of its hero, this reviewer (and others) warmly, often sentimentally, welcomed back the fictional world that Thackeray had created. This extra long gap between installments underscores the effects of serial publication: through the long months of reading—of the reader's, author's, and characters' association—critical objectivity decreased and a sense of shared life increased. The rhetorical tone of the review ("smitten like a child at play," "lost to us for a while," "the darkness and stillness of the sick-chamber") sug-

55

gests the intensity of the serial reader's identification with the world of the fictional characters. The Victorian parts reader carried the world of the novel into his own, real world, expanding and extending key elements of the author's creation to meet deeply felt personal and societal needs. The continued appearance of *Pendennis*, its hero and his company, reinforced the reader's awareness of his own continued existence, his success or his failure, his growth or decay. In a sense, the serial novel became a clock for the reader, measuring his movement through this world.

Thackeray's achievement in *Pendennis*, then, deserves increased recognition. He chronicles his protagonist's evolution from naive provincial youth to sophisticated London literary man and husband, avoiding some aspects of the conventional bildungsroman formula because of his belief in the stability of character through time. Thackeray, however, takes special advantage of the dominant nineteenth-century genre—the serial novel—to further his protagonist's growth in the twenty-five month length of his bildungsroman. By stressing the passing of time in the reader's experience through a variety of narrative techniques, Thackeray keeps his protagonist always in motion in the eyes of his observer. The sense of development or change is consistently a part of reading Thackeray in 1848–50, even though Pen may not be changing swiftly or dramatically in any one monthly installment. Even between parts, the reader's time is used to expand or extend key elements of the novel.

Although Thackeray, like some of his contemporaries and other novelists later in the century, felt some frustration with the process of serial composition—insisting, for instance, that his next novel, *Henry Esmond* (1852), not appear in parts—his major accomplishments are in that mode: *Vanity Fair* (1847–48) and *The Newcomes* (1853–55). Reading the monthly issue of a nineteenth-century serial novel, by Thackeray, Dickens, Eliot, or another, meant two things to its readers: an extended life for the characters of that world (Rebecca Sharp, Arthur Pendennis, and Ethel Newcome continue to grow up); and an ongoing life for the readers (who are growing up also). Thackeray's narrative skills are revealed in his

56

ability to engage the reader's real existence (part of the novel's context) to supplement the fictional existence of his own creation (the novel's text). Before going on to discuss the different experience of reading Thackeray's successful three-volume novel *Henry Esmond*, I wish to continue the exploration of reading *Pendennis*, examining in particular how the January 1850 debate in the Victorian periodical press about the nature of literature became a significant part of Thackeray's bildungsroman.

3
Novels, Writers, and Readers in 1850

In October, November, and December 1849 William Makepeace Thackeray was ill, and the appearance of number 12 in his serialized bildungsroman, *Pendennis,* was delayed from October 1849 to January 1850. Number 11 of *Pendennis* (September 1849) had included fictional portraits of authors who had some ability but sold their talent to publishers of little education and less integrity. This unfavorable picture of literary London had a particularly long life in its original format, extending three times the length of the usual gap between installments. During this break in the text, one body of Thackeray's readers, writers for the periodical press, took up the question of the author's place in a modern society. This public discussion in turn inspired significant responses on Thackeray's part in the composition of the remaining numbers of his fiction. The following question raised by his hero in August 1849 (the novel's number 10), then, later received a detailed answer from Thackeray: ". . . but how is one to live? . . . There is beef and bread in plenty in England, but you must pay for it with work or money. And who will take my work? and what work can I do?"

This same debate about the literary profession also had its effect on a second major novelist of the period. When the gap in *Pendennis* occurred, Charles Dickens had published six parts of his fictional autobiography, *David Copperfield;* and the debate in the Victorian press about the role of writers became an important influence in the future of Dickens's hero, as David becomes in the end a writer of fiction. In the final installment of Dickens's text, Copperfield asserts: "I resolved to remain away from home for some time longer; to settle myself for the present in Switzerland, which was growing dear to me . . . to resume my pen: to work." In their art at the middle of the century Dickens and Thackeray attempted to broaden their audience's understanding of the novelist's place in society.

In a three-month period at the very end of 1849, then, we can document in unusual detail how one set of historical readers (writers for the periodical press) responded to specific literary texts (Thackeray's *Pendennis* and Dickens's *Copperfield*). We can identify, that is, "actual" as well as "implied" readers. "Implied" readers are found, as Wolfgang Iser has explained, by examining the "role" that "the real reader is always offered . . . to play" by the text; and actual readers reflect "the way in which a literary work has been received by a specific reading public."[1] In the discussion that follows, I cite contemporary reactions to two mid-Victorian novels in an effort to define an actual historical reader; and I pursue Iser's method of examining the texts to identify the implied reader in the same novels.

The dialectic between writer (in this case, Thackeray) and reader (reviewers for the periodical press) is related to what Iser terms "the wandering viewpoint" in literary experience. He asserts that "the basic hermeneutic structure of reading" involves anticipation and memory: "every moment of reading is a dialectic of protension and retention, conveying a future horizon yet to be occupied, along with a past (and continually fading) horizon already filled; the wandering viewpoint carves its passage through both at the same time and leaves them to merge together in its wake" (p. 112). Thackeray's number 9, with its unflattering portrait of authors in January 1850, may be viewed as a "past horizon"; the periodical press's response to Thackeray's text can be considered a "future horizon." As Thackeray in turn responds, through the composition of additional numbers of *Pendennis,* to this criticism, and as Dickens enters the same debate about the role of writers, we can begin to chart the course of a Victorian "wandering viewpoint" at the middle of the century. As multiple definitions of the writer are considered, we can see how reading Thackeray meant revising and refining essential cultural values.

The approach of citing Victorian periodical response to document consideration of the author's standing in society helps to counter one complaint about reader-oriented criticism, that it is theoretical and subjective. In *The Reader in the Text: Essays on Audience and Interpretation* (Princeton: Princeton Univ. Press, 1980), for instance, Susan R. Suleiman describes Wolfgang Iser's phenomenological approach to reading with one clear reservation: "it is important to note that the individual subject it [Iser's method] poses is often indistinguishable from an abstract and generalized 'reader'" (p. 26). Although Iser drew a line between a contemporary reader of a work of art (a participant) and a later reader (an observer), Suleiman insists "we are still dealing with implied, not actual, readers. . . . the description of each one's response remains schematic and general" (p. 26). In *Reader-Response Criticism: From Formalism to Post-Structuralism* (Baltimore: John Hopkins Univ. Press, 1980), Jane P. Tompkins argues that "meaning [in literary experience] is a consequence of being in a particular situation in the world"; thus, to identify any "particular" situation is to give substance to a theoretical reader (p. xxv). One particular moment in the Victorian period, October–December 1849, then, supplies an opportunity for studying a group of actual readers in comparison with the implied readers of two major authors.[2] We can see in this moment a dynamic evolving relationship between writer and reader, as, in the course of novels' publication, authors and audience move toward new understandings of important values in their world.[3]

An editorial in the *Morning Chronicle* (3 January 1850) objected to Thackeray's "fostering a baneful prejudice" against the profession of letters in the eleven installments of his novel published to that point. The larger concern of the editorial, however—state support of literature in the form of pensions for writers—revealed a more equivocal attitude toward writers and their place in society. Throughout the essay ran a typical Victorian insistence on laissez-faire in literary as in all matters: "Protection to literature or science is mischievous in nearly the same way as protection to commerce. The let-alone system is equally desireable for both. In an immense majority of instances, the genius which deserves to be encouraged does not wait for or require encouragement; and its self-dependence—its capacity for making its own way against all obstacles—is the best criterion of its genuineness." Although genius will ultimately gain monetary reward for its efforts, the editorial's conclusion suggested that the real reward for such great men was less material. If the place of genius in the usual system of production was somewhat vague here, the position of less-than-immortal authors seems curiously associated with a state of poverty: "All we would venture to throw out for public consideration is—whether poverty, coupled with ordinary merit, in a man of letters, should be deemed a sufficient title to national aid; whether, on the contrary, such aid should be conferred at all, unless as the spontaneous expression of national gratitude, as the promise and fore-runner of immortality." Also, according to the editorial, writers who are less than immortal do very little real work: "the love of notoriety inherent in mankind, combined with the common distaste for continuous or unexciting labour, will always attract an undue number of recruits from other employments to literature." Thus, most writers do something less than work, in the *Chronicle*'s view, because they are not involved in continuous and unexciting exertion. Such figures, who sought the financial support of the state, became, in one of the more biting phrases of the editorial, "literary paupers," a class that was surely a detriment to society.

The *Morning Chronicle*'s view—that men of letters as a class were lazy and unable to compete in an open market—was not an uncommon one for its time. In May 1851, the *Prospective Review*, in an essay about both *Copperfield* and *Pendennis,* made a clear distinction between authorship and those professions that required work: "David Copperfield and Pendennis are both men who have left the beaten path of the professions to devote themselves to literature"

(p. 159). The article also complained that Pen was an undisciplined character because he had escaped the "necessity of making a livelihood in a regular way" (p. 172). In a review of *Copperfield* in December 1850, *Fraser's* complained half-seriously: "But then these authors are always lazy, and rarely work without the devil at their elbow, waiting for—copy" (p. 701). Even in David Masson's favorable and influential review of both novels (*North British Review*, May 1851) we see the notion that art ought to be above economic concerns, that the products of genius are lessened when they are recognized as work through the payment of money:

> Our writers of fiction, for the most part, candidly own that they write to make money and amuse people. Their merit is therefore the greater, when, like the two eminent writers whose works we have been discussing, they do more than this. Should we suggest that their functions would be intrinsically higher, and more satisfactory to their own better judgment, did they work less according to the external demand, and more according to the internal wish and form, they will admit the suggestion to the full, but say that on the whole they are not strong enough to follow it. (Pp. 88–89)

Such assertions by the *Morning Chronicle* and others that literature in general and novels in particular constituted a unique profession, involving little work and requiring no material reward, seemed to hit home in the literary community of 1850. Not only did Dickens and Thackeray respond to these ideas through their ongoing novels, but Dickens's close friend, John Forster, also openly attempted to counter them through essays in the periodical press. In an editorial in the *Examiner* two days later, Forster argued that state pensions for authors were actually a reasonable payment for services rendered: "There is no parallel between commercial protection and the recognition of services done to the State by literary men. Services done to the State by distinguished efforts in art, literature, and science, are as unequivocal, and at least as important, as services done by professors of arms, law, divinity, and diplomacy" (p. 2). Forster thus accepted the *Morning Chronicle*'s argument that literature was distinct among the professions, but drew a different conclusion. He admitted that the "votaries of commerce are best left to pursue their speculations uninterfered with by Government. Gain is the object of their efforts. . . ." However, Forster went on to say, "in acquiring scholastic treasures the man of letters is more likely to miss than to obtain the means of providing against daily wants." Here, and in a later editorial, "The Dignity of Literature" (the *Examiner,* 19 January 1850), Forster insisted that the economic system of the time failed to reward fairly the writer's efforts: "We say that the disposition to concede to it [literature] a position thus proportioned to its rights has not yet been shown by our rulers and governors, nor exhibited by any class of the community" (p. 35). Thus, Forster argued that literature was a profession as valid as any other; that writers did perform work worthy of earnings; but that the state must supply that reward because the "let-alone" system had failed to do so. As I will attempt to show later, most of Forster's points were pursued by his friend Dickens in *David Copperfield.* A different point of view, simultaneously presented by Dickens's rival Thackeray, deserves attention as well.

Thackeray's initial response to the *Morning Chronicle's* charges, in a letter to the editor published on 12 January 1850, took a different approach to the issue from Forster's. Thackeray argued that writers were adequately recognized by society, but he laced the argument with ironies that could be noted by the readers of his novels: "That generous faith in men of letters, that kindly regard in which the whole reading nation holds them, appear to me to be so clearly shown in our country every day, that to question them would be as absurd as, permit me to say for my part, it would be ungrateful."[4] Even as Thackeray admitted that the rewards writers received were not necessarily monetary ones, he indirectly asserted that the system did not always recognize quality: "The rewards of the profession are not to be measured by the money-standard; for one man spends a life of learning and labour on a book which does not pay the printer's bill and another gets a little fortune by a few light volumes. But putting the money out of the question, I believe that the social estimation of the man of letters is as good as it deserves to be, and as good as that of any other professional man" (p. 632). Thackeray seemed to intend in this letter to lessen the force of the *Morning Chronicle*'s criticism of the literary class by agreeing with them, but by also inviting his readers to read between the lines: "instead of accusing the public of persecuting and disparaging us as a class, it seems to me that men of letters had best silently assume that they are as good as any other gentlemen; nor raise piteous controversies upon a question which all people of sense must take to be settled" (p. 634).

This letter to the *Morning Chronicle*, of course, was Thackeray's public voice speaking directly to his readers; his words in private reinforced an ironic perspective on the debate. In a letter to Abraham Hayward written less than two weeks later, Thackeray admitted: "The words in Pendennis are untenable be hanged to them; but they were meant to apply to a particular class of literary men, *my* class who are the most ignorant men under the Sun, myself included I mean. But I wrote so carelessly that it appears as if I would speak of all, & even if it were true I ought never to have written what I did. . . ."[5] As I will show, in the ongoing form of his fictional bildungsroman, Thackeray attempted to alter this image of the Victorian artist he regretted in private having endorsed. Thackeray's public acceptance of conventional nineteenth-century concepts of the literary profession and Forster's criticism of these concepts, however, are both linked to a second issue having to do with writers in the 1840s: the effort to establish a "society of authors," an organization of writers that would openly negotiate for their rights in the larger economic system. Before considering in detail the late numbers of *Pendennis* and *Copperfield*, which came after the *Morning Chronicle*'s editorial and the ensuing debate, I wish to review briefly the place of novelists in the economic system prior to 1850.

The most significant effort to initiate a bargaining force for writers, in 1843, was linked to the long battle to establish the principles of copyright, which resulted in five significant parliamentary acts between 1833 and 1855. The influential forces behind the copyright movement were, of course, the publishers, whose goal

65

throughout the century was an international copyright agreement forcing foreign competitors to pay for the right to reprint British books, something not achieved until 1866. From the authors' point of view, though, the most important of these five acts was the Copyright Amendment Act of 1842, which extended the author's term of copyright, "with a statutory protection period of forty-two years from publication or till seven years from the death of the author, whichever was longer."[6] Before this time, the generally accepted view of the author's role in the sale of his works derived from the belief that, although a manuscript was the exclusive property of the writer, once it was sold to a publisher, the publisher could produce and sell actual books, which were his exclusive property. After 1842 the principle of the author's ownership—not only of the manuscript but also of the work of art—was more firmly established. The bill specifically referred to literary works as "the Property of such Author," and included the larger social justification for recognizing this right: "it is expedient . . . to afford greater Encouragement to the Production of Literary Works of lasting Benefit to the World. . . ."[7] Those who opposed this bill, by the way, argued that copyright was a "tax on readers for the purpose of giving a bounty to writers,"[8] an argument not unlike the *Morning Chronicle*'s objection to state pensions for authors in 1850.

Although the 1842 act clearly advanced some rights of authors, it confused others, as John Sutherland has noted: "did an agreement between author and publisher constitute a 'sale of copyright' or merely the assignation of a 'privilege to print and publish'? This had the baffling complexity of a metaphysical problem for literary minds of the day. Who actually 'owned' property was never stated on contracts after the Copyright Amendment Act of 1842."[9] In such an atmosphere of uncertainty, as Victor Bonham-Carter has reported in *Authors by Profession*, a group of prominent authors, called by Bulwer-Lytton and including Dickens, met in March 1843, to discuss the possibilities for joint effort. After a second meeting in April, attended by both Thackeray and Dickens, a letter was sent to potential members, stating that a goal of the projected organization would be "To secure the observance of the laws for the protection of authors and their property."[10] Almost as quickly as the idea of a "society of authors" was raised in 1843, however, it faded away. In a letter to potential members on 27 April, Dickens, the most powerful because most successful individual of the group, withdrew his support, admitting that ". . . I approved of the Design in theory, but in practice considered it hopeless."[11] Dickens clearly felt that organization apart from publishers would be ineffective: he recognized their "wealth, business habits, and interests" to be "of great importance."[12] He supported the forming of an "Association for the Protection of Literature" on 16 May, which was open to all elements of the book trade. This latter group was functioning, although without great effect, as late as 1849, the year *Copperfield* and *Pendennis* appeared.

The reasons urging the formation of such organizations in the 1840s is clear: authors as a class had generally no power in an economic system dominated by publishers. Like those in the same years involved in the Ten-hours Movement and the Chartist Movement, they were seeking their place in a new, unregulated economic system.[13] One of the chief reasons for the failures of such groups to gain ground was clearly the relationship of author to publisher. As John Sutherland pointed out, both classes of men "were cultivated and charming people in the main; not surprisingly when business threw them together they tended to stay together as friends."[14] Since publishers controlled the business of literature, authors found it difficult, both personally and professionally, to organize in a way that would appear to be in opposition to that group. Another of the reasons was the image of authors most Victorians held at this time. In the public mind, novelists were hacks who worked for publishers;[15] publishers, on the other hand, produced, owned, and sold literary property as regular businessmen, even after the Copyright Amendment Act of 1842. Those who supported the organization of authors recognized that the climate was not yet right for effective political action in such laissez-faire times: Harriet Martineau wrote to a friend that what was needed was "mutual assistance to extricate us from the transition state between old patronage, and that free communication between speakers and hearers—

67

writers and readers—which must be arrived at sooner or later."[16] George Henry Lewes indicated more specifically what path authors must follow toward freedom from old world patronage, represented by the Royal Literary Fund, and new style control by publishers, which was still crucial in the Association for the Protection of Literature: "Opinion must first be influenced, and then the organization of a profession will evolve itself from the opinion. . . ."[17]

In 1849 and 1850, recalling the recent revolutions in Europe and witnessing continued Chartist agitation at home, the public's mood demanded stability for an increasingly successful British system. Authors recognized that they could not organize politically to combat the system any more than they had in 1843; but they could begin to encourage the people who might later allow them economic independence to see the literary profession in new lights. After the sudden manifestation of public opinion about British writers in the January 1850 *Morning Chronicle* editorial, Dickens and Thackeray could respond with their own image of the novelist in the remaining installments of their current serial novels, *David Copperfield* and *Pendennis*. In Iser's terms, the "implied reader" of these texts would recognize the value of the artist to society. As the "actual" historical reader read on through 1850, he would be encouraged to shift his position toward that of the "implied reader."

To attempt to alter the conventional Victorian notion of the artist, Thackeray in particular had material at hand in 1849–50. In number 10 of *Pendennis* (August 1849) the protagonist had met George Warrington, the man who would help him earn a living as an author. Although Warrington himself admitted he didn't "wish it to be said that George Warrington writes for bread,"[18] his embarrassment about membership in the literary profession was countered in the novel by his friend's youthful optimism. When Pen received his first check from the publisher Bacon, he was "as elated as if somebody had left him a fortune" (1:317). His enthusiasm forced the admission from Warrington, "Well, you may get bread and cheese, Pen: and I own it tastes well, the bread which you earn yourself." These two fictional characters, referred to by one acquaintance as "Mr. Pennington" (1:324)—one young and naive, the other experienced and pragmatic—together present Thackeray's image of the Victorian writer as one whose art grew out of suffering, and who must labor to achieve economic self-sufficiency.[19] Thackeray's "implied reader," of course, appreciated the qualities of "Mr. Pennington" and acted from this point in the novel as a model for Thackeray's "actual reader" (represented in the *Morning Chronicle* editorial).

Thackeray, as narrator of the two writers' story, insisted through use of the first-person plural at the beginning of number 12 (January 1850) that his readers recognize how the literary profession, like all others, involved regular toil:

> . . . . we know how the life of any hack, legal or literary, in a curacy, or in a marching regiment, or at a merchant's desk, is full of routine, and tedious of description. One day's labour resembles another much too closely. A literary man has often to work for his bread against time, or against his will, or in spite of his health, or of his indolence, of his repugnance to the subject on which he is called to exert himself, just like any other daily toiler. When you want to make money by Pegasus, (as he must, perhaps, who has no other saleable property), farewell poetry and aerial flights. . . . (1:353)

Giving a brief account of the composition of *Walter Lorraine,* Pen's first novel, the narrator insisted on the difficulty of any writer's creating: "If the secret history of books could be written, and the author's private thoughts and meanings noted down alongside of his story, how many insipid volumes would become interesting, and dull tales excite the reader!" (2:22). The "reader" at the end of this sentence is clearly Thackeray's "implied reader." As Warrington was quick to agree, Pen was no "Homer, Æschylus, [or] Shakespeare" (2:24), but his efforts should be respected: when Pen dramatically pretended to throw the early manuscript version of his experiences into the fire, both he and Warrington knew it was "uncommonly clever," worthy of exchange "for money" (2:27). Even with success, however, both Pen and Warrington have to work consistently in Thackeray's fictional portrayal of the Victorian

69

world of letters: "the excitement of literary composition pretty soon subsides with the hired labourer . . . So, indeed, Mr. Arthur performed his work at the Pall Mall Gazette, (and since his success as a novelist with an increased salary,) but without the least enthusiasm, doing his best or pretty nearly, and sometimes writing ill and sometimes well. He was a literary hack, naturally fast in pace, and brilliant in action" (2:92).

When Pen fell ill later in the novel, Warrington could take over his friend's editorial responsibilities because he, even more than Pen, had learned to be a productive worker: "In a word, Warrington went to work with all his might, in place of his prostrate friend, and did Pen's portion of the 'Pall Mall Gazette' 'with a vengeance,' as the saying is. He wrote occasional articles and literary criticisms; he attended theatres and musical performances, and discoursed about them with his usual savage energy" (2:141). By the final number of the novel, it seemed appropriate to Thackeray's reader that Warrington had stayed up all night to finish his work, and that the result was the betterment of society:

> The labour was done, and the night was worn away somehow, and the tardy November dawn came and looked in on the young man as he sate over his desk. In the next day's paper, or quarter's review, many of us very likely admired the work of his genius, the variety of his illustration, the fierce vigour of his satire, the depth of his reason. . . . We have said before, could we know the man's feelings as well as the author's thoughts—how interesting most books would be!—more interesting than merry. I suppose harlequin's face behind his mask is always grave, if not melancholy—certainly each man who lives by the pen, and happens to read this, must remember, if he will, his own experiences and recall many solemn hours of solitude and labour." (2:321–22).

Again, the "implied reader" is this sentence's "each man."

With his professional integrity, Warrington did become one of the favorites of the novel's actual audience, as a review in the *Spectator* revealed:

. . . it is no very rare thing among that class [England's "better class of young men"] to find the best scholars and the truest gentlemen neither too fine to drink beer and smoke short pipes, nor too delicate to have the will and the power to thrash bargemen when occasion demands. In England, where to rise by one's own exertion requires such a combination of physical and mental power, and where the national idea leans rather to strength than subtlety, to sense than to learning, to rank plainness of manners and of speech and kindness of heart than to stately courtesy and elaborate polish, many a dignitary of church and law, and many a man eminent for social and political success, might have supplied the oddest as well as the noblest traits of Warrington's character.[20]

Another early review similarly praised Warrington for "acting the part of an honest and strong-minded guide of public opinion, disciplining his mind by severe though intermittent study, and gaining his livelihood by supplying his readers with valuable facts and ideas on subjects which he understood better than they."[21] The blend of aristocratic learning and middle-class effort in Warrington's character suggests that Thackeray knew the qualities his actual readers would appreciate, and that through the model of his own "implied reader" he hoped to encourage them to think better of the Victorian writer.

It is not only in two writers' steady application to their tasks that Thackeray's fiction attempted to revise the actual reader's understanding of literary production. The youthful Pen, just entering the writer's profession in number 11 of the novel, objects strenuously to the publisher's role in the business of books: "No man shall tell me that a man of genius, as Shandon is, ought to be driven by such a vulgar slave driver, as yonder Mr. Bungay, whom we have just left, who fattens on the profits of the other's brains, and enriches himself out of his journeyman's labour." Although Warrington insisted that it was Shandon's own improvidence that enslaved him to a capitalist-publisher, he, too, recognized that writers as a group had grievances: "So you have begun already to gird at the publishers, and to take your side amongst our order. Bravo, Pen my

71

boy!" (1:327). A second outburst against the apparent injustices of the system recalls the debate over the Copyright Amendment Act of 1842 and the thoughts of writers then who envisioned a society of authors: "I protest against that wretch of a middle-man whom I see between Genius and his great landlord, the Public, and who stops more than half of the labourer's earnings and fame" (1:328). It is perhaps this specific attack on the role of publishers in the book trade—even though softened by Warrington in the ensuing dialogue—that led to the *Morning Chronicle*'s editorial. It undermined the conviction that the Victorian laissez-faire economy justly rewarded authors and publishers. It is to his credit that in subsequent numbers of the novel Thackeray did not alter his characterization of Bacon and Bungay, the two publishers; instead he tended to strengthen his portrait of "Pennington" as a hardworking, instructive, humane professional.

In his long apprenticeship in the literary profession, of course, Thackeray himself had learned the lessons of hard work. One review of *Pendennis* suggested that Thackeray had also earned the respect of his "actual" audience in his labour: "Buried for many and many a year in the great deeps of the weekly and monthly periodicals, William Makepeace Thackeray has only of late emerged upon the light of day and with so sure a requital for his long disappearance that he is now a counter-capitalist—with the most popular of English writers [Dickens]. . . ."[22] Robert Colby's recent study of Thackeray reinforces this image of the successful artist in the highest Victorian manner: "Thackeray emerges as a remarkable example of a recurrent Victorian type, the high popularizer, who answered . . . to the needs of a serious kind of reader who had emerged in the nineteenth century, the cultural aspirant, and catered to the strong desire for 'improvement' encouraged by adult educators—clerical and lay."[23] In this effort to be and to describe the Victorian author/teacher, Thackeray was being helped during the months of *Pendennis*'s publication by the most successful novelist of his time, Charles Dickens.

As Thackeray's portrait of Pendennis and Warrington is a reaction to conventional ideas of the novelist, visible in the *Morning*

72

Chronicle editorial, Dickens's decision to make his character David Copperfield an author may be a much more direct response to his actual readers than has been recognized. And Dickens's response to the debate, of which *Pendennis*'s first eleven numbers are one source, in the end impinges on the thirteen numbers of Thackeray's novel published thereafter. Reading Thackeray in January 1850 and later becomes, that is, a matter also of reading Dickens, as the full context of public debate about the role of the author helps create the meaning of *Pendennis*.

To recover the effect of Dickens's novel on Thackeray's (and vice versa), we must abandon a more modern concept of the author in favor of Victorian standards. Philip Collins has noted that modern readers have generally found the adult David Copperfield unconvincing: "It was a mistake for Dickens to make his hero a novelist if, for whatever reasons, he felt so reluctant to flesh out the assertion that David succeeded in this line. . . . Dickens plays false here to the art he professed, for he well knew how much self-commitment beyond 'my strongest earnestness' goes into creation: and if 'every energy of my soul' was exerted, such an effort obviously deserved more detailed attention in a novel purporting to be about its hero's 'Personal History and Experience.' "[24] In demanding a fuller presentation of Dickens's hero as author, Collins and others may be underestimating the force of the ideology which dominated Dickens's "actual reader." The many twentieth-century portraits of the artist have developed a thoroughly detailed image of the writer for modern readers. In 1850, the year in which *Copperfield* and *Pendennis* were coming out in parts, Wordsworth's *The Prelude,* or "The Growth of a Poet's Mind," was just appearing. As Maurice Beebe pointed out, *David Copperfield* was "the first portrait of the artist in English fiction that stands up in its own right as a major work of art."[25] Since, as Collins also reminded us, there was "widespread agreement that Copperfield was [Dickens's] masterpiece,"[26] the hero's representation of a novelist probably conformed to rather than boldly contradicted Victorian standards; but it still helped shape a new awareness of the writer's relationship to other men.

The modern complaint about Dickens's portrait of the artist is one of the reasons Victorians admired it: Copperfield is "earnest." Angus Wilson said in 1970 that the "philistine, bourgeois, complacent view of his powers as a writer only reflects the social and ethical whole of the book."[27] On the other hand, *Blackwood's Magazine* in 1855 admired Dickens's characterization of his protagonist: "All about him is so quiet, and real, and free from exaggeration," including his appearance "as author."[28] The Victorian notion of the writer as literary pauper that Dickens was reacting to after the *Morning Chronicle* editorial inspired David's many affirmations of middle-class values, just as it did Pendennis's: "I never could have done what I have done, without the habits of punctuality, order, and diligence . . ." (p. 428; June 1850).[29] The same qualities that served him as proctor and stenographer contributed to his performance as novelist: "my [literary] success had steadily increased with my steady application" (p. 471; July 1950), he later admitted. The moral effect of his labors is the same as Thackeray found in Warrington's effort: Agnes told David, "'Your growing reputation and success enlarge your power of doing good . . .'" (p. 599; November 1850). Thus, the kind of novelist Dickens allowed David Copperfield to become was meant to revise conventional Victorian ideas about the literary profession by showing him as, fundamentally, a hard worker. The "implied reader" who appreciated Copperfield's earnestness was the model for the novel's "actual" reader. While this image does not appeal to our modern tastes, it certainly did to the Victorians'.

There is perhaps an even closer connection between David Copperfield and the Victorian stereotype: it may be that Dickens's decision to have his hero become a novelist was a direct response to the debate about the profession waged by Thackeray, the *Morning Chronicle,* and Dickens's friend John Forster. Much of the story of *Copperfield's* composition has been told, first by Forster and later by Butt and Tillotson, among others;[30] but whether Dickens knew from the outset that his hero would become a novelist or made that decision during publication has not been established. Dickens had written in 1845–48 a portion of an autobiography; but *Copperfield* was begun in the early months of 1849 as a separate venture, and the autobiographical material was only used later, primarily in July 1849, for the novel's fourth number, as part of David's story. In its original title and subsequent variations, no clue is given that the hero might ultimately become a novelist.[31] The title under which the first number appeared, unlike *The History of Pendennis*, offered no suggestion of a literary future: *The Personal History, Adventures, Experience, and Observation of David Copperfield the Younger, of Blunderstone Rockery, Which He never meant to be Published on any Account.* As Robert Patten has pointed out, the reluctance to appear in print seems particularly uncharacteristic of a novelist.[32] If we adopt a later date for Dickens's decision to have David become a writer, we may be able to shed some additional light on the inconsistencies of his adult character and ultimately add to the context that shaped Victorian understanding of Thackeray's *Pendennis* in 1848–50.

The gap in *Pendennis*'s publication—October 1849 through January 1850—may have provided the impetus for Dickens to settle on novel writing as his hero's final profession. During those months Dickens was working on numbers 7, 8, and 9 of *Copperfield,* in which David goes to work in London as a proctor in the firm of Spenlow and Jorkins.[33] The direction David's life was to take after his schooling at Doctor Strong's apparently gave Dickens some trouble during the months of October and November. Butt and Tillotson explain that on 15 November "he was still . . . turning over in his mind a suitable profession for David".[34] According to Forster's account of that period, Dickens considered David as a "special pleader" and in a "banking" career. On 17 November, though, he rejected banking because he thought it would slow up the story. He wrote to Forster, "I have taken, for the present at all events, the proctor" as David's profession.[35] Whether Dickens's "for the present" indicates that he already knew David would become a novelist later or that he was unsure about the whole question of David's career at this point is unclear; but it is evident that he was turning over in his mind possibilities for his hero's profession during the months that Thackeray's portrait of the literary profession (*Pendennis*'s October number) was on the Victorian mind. That portrait had bothered Dickens's friend Forster to the extent that he wrote two editorials for the *Examiner* to correct Thackeray's version of the Victorian writer. It may be that Dickens—sometime between November 1849 and May 1850— decided to add to Forster's efforts through his own fiction by having David Copperfield become a novelist, an author who was also a regular Victorian businessman. Maurice Beebe admits that "the development of David as artist seems dependent more on an accident of circumstances than on nature," but then is able to find characteristics of the literary type in David's childhood personality.[36] It may be, however, that Dickens turned a sensitive character into a novelist in the course of the novel's composition and publication. The current critical opinion, expressed by Robert Patten and others,[37] that Dickens was perhaps unconsciously working out an understanding of himself as novelist through the writing of *Copperfield* does not contradict such a theory about the sequence of events in 1849–50.

Despite the fact that both Dickens and Thackeray did react through their art to unfavorable ideas about novelists, there are other signs that their efforts to change public opinion are circumscribed by their own historical situation. The evolution of Warrington, Pendennis, and Copperfield as authors after the *Morning Chronicle* editorial, while positive in general, still contained some uncertainty, like Warrington's embarrassment at making his living by writing. The fact that the creative process and its products are never described in much detail in either *Pendennis* or *Copperfield* does underscore an uneasiness with this subject matter, leading almost to an apology for the writer's efforts, for his "private thoughts and feelings" in the "secret history of books" (*Pendennis* 2:22). Such strains in the narrative, existing in counterpoint to the primary insistence on the author's social contribution, show that Dickens and Thackeray, even as they composed successive numbers of their serial novels in the effort to enlighten their readers, were themselves evaluating and revising their own understanding of the novelist in society. Their own need to succeed as writers, in part by pleasing their subscribers, may well have been a factor in their reluctance to assault accepted values without reserve. Thackeray, in fact, was financially secure as a writer only after the publication of *Pendennis*.[38] Dickens, in writing *Copperfield*, tried to maintain his popularity in the literary world against Thackeray, the first substantial rival of his career.[39]

More significantly, it seems clear now that in rejecting one stereotype of the artist Dickens and Thackeray were adopting another with its own contradictory connotations for the future. In an article on Dickens's involvement in social causes during his career, N. N. Feltes has argued persuasively that writers, like the rest of the Victorian population, were caught up in forces of change even they could not understand fully at the time. He reminds us, for example, that the Factory Act of 1853, which finally defined the "normal working day," was as much a compromise as the victory many workers believed it to be: if they had won the right to spend their time off the job as they pleased, workers had given to their employers a right to govern their hours on the job.[40] Similarly, novelists fighting for economic bargaining power in 1850 had given up a romantic notion of the writer as unconscious, effortless creator for the image of hardworking bourgeois businessman. They did not seem conscious of the constraints such a stereotype would place on writers in subsequent generations who would no longer enthusiastically endorse the conventions of Victorian earnestness. For Henry James and most of the novelists who came after him, the writers's first step toward great art would be the rejection of middle-class values.

At midcentury, however, Thackeray and Dickens were the two major authors competing for the attention of middle-class audiences. *David Copperfield* and *Pendennis*, appearing simultaneously in 1849–50, share many traits: each is a long bildungsroman whose hero survives youthful infatuation and loss of wealth to become a successful man of letters married to an angelic woman. As the beginning sentences of David Masson's influential review, *"Pendennis* and *Copperfield:* Thackeray *and* Dickens," suggest, readers may have tended to see one world in these two works: "Thackeray and Dickens, Dickens and Thackeray—the two names now almost necessarily go together . . . the public has learned to think of them in

77

indissoluble connexion. . . . As the popular novelists of the day, Dickens and Thackeray, and again, Thackeray and Dickens, divide the public attention" (*North British Review,* May 1851). In other words, Thackeray, Dickens, and their actual readers were creating at this time a literary model of evolving Victorian ideology. Within that construct, Dickens and Thackeray, through the effects of their "implied readers," were winning a new place of respectability for novels and novelists at midcentury; but the exact nature of that place and its influence on the shape of art for the future was not yet clear. How much they had gained for their profession and what they had lost is to be measured in the relationship of later novelists to their actual readers. We need to look next to the evolving shapes of the "implied readers" in the installments of later nineteenth-century novels and to the responses of actual readers in the periodicals of the day. We will find there, I believe, the same kind of shifting, evolving relationship between author and readers that we see between Thackeray (or Dickens) and his audience in 1850; but in pursuing the study of installment readers and texts of major serial novelists we can trace in more detail the history of important ideas like the novelist's place in society throughout the Victorian age.

Before Thackeray continues the exploration and alteration of Victorian ideas in the serial mode, however, he turns his attention to another subject and another format: the nature of history, and the three-volume novel. *Henry Esmond* (1852) involves a fundamentally different kind of reading than that inspired by what in Thackeray's career precedes it, *Pendennis* (1848–50), and what follows it, *The Newcomes* (1853–55). It thus becomes an excellent "control" in this study of reading Thackeray. *Esmond* demonstrates how context shapes text by deliberately separating itself to a much greater degree than his other works from the contemporary setting in which author and audience find themselves.

4
Building the House of Esmond

George Henry Lewes wrote in the *Leader* on 6 November 1852 that he found *Henry Esmond* "as unlike *Vanity Fair* and *Pendennis* as a book written by Thackeray can be."[1] Part of his response is due, of course, to the eighteenth-century subject and style of Thackeray's third major novel. Writing in the *Times,* Samuel Phillips was dismayed to see "the distinguished novelist, whose very breath of life is the atmosphere in which he lives, and whose most engaging quality is his own natural style, had suicidally determined to convey himself to a strange climate and to take absolute leave of his choicest characteristics."[2] Both commentators were acknowledging how much the Victorian public had been involved in Thackeray's earlier publications because their subjects had been the contemporary Victorian scene. As much as subject matter, however, publication format made reading *Esmond* different. As a three-volume work, *Esmond* was more an object to be engaged by each individual in a private reading than a social phenomenon involving a continuing dialogue between author and audience. In *Vanity Fair* and *Pendennis* the serial format had specifically given the audience time, in the space between numbers, to savor their feelings and voice their opinions about characters and events before Thackeray continued the story.

Wolfgang Iser in *The Act of Reading* (Baltimore: Johns Hopkins Univ. Press, 1978) provides a critical framework that can be used to assess some aspects of the reading situation inspired by a three-volume work. He makes the observation that we cannot grasp the whole of any text, particularly a long one:

> Large-scale texts such as novels or epics cannot be continually 'present' to the reader with an identical degree of intensity. . . . A typical instance of this is the metaphor used by Fielding, Scott, and others, whereby the reader is likened to a traveler in a stagecoach, who has to make the often difficult journey through the novel, gazing out from his moving viewpoint. Naturally, he combines all that he sees within his memory and establishes a pattern of consistency, the nature and reliability of which will depend partly on the degree of attention he has paid during each phase of the journey. At no time, however, can he have a total view of that journey. (p. 16)

More time necessarily passes in the journey of reading a twenty-part serial text than it does when a three-volume novel is read at a single or a few sittings. In describing what happens during the prolonged experiences of installment reading, I have made use of Iser's concept of the "wandering viewpoint" (see chap. 3), arguing that expectations about what might happen at any moment in the literary experience are expanded by the context of the readers' world in the space between numbers. To explain what happens in the case of the three-volume *Esmond*, however, I will focus more on what Iser terms "consistency-building," the reader's selection of elements of the text and fitting them into a basic, encompassing pattern of understanding (pp. 125–26).

While both the wandering viewpoint and consistency-building are inevitably aspects of any literary experience (as Iser's detailed readings of individual texts demonstrate), the distinct mode of serial reading allows, I believe, for freer play of the wandering viewpoint; in works read essentially all at once the process of consistency-building is, by contrast, stronger. By opposing the operation of the wandering viewpoint in an eighteen-month installment reading experience with the consistency-building of reading an entire work essentially all at once, I am attempting to write large two major activities in any literary event.

In analyzing consistency-building—that is, identifying what elements of a text's response remain within an audience's basic formulation of meaning—I am concentrating on the role of memory in reading, on what happens after the experience of reading individual sentences or whole novels. Victorians in their evaluation and understanding of Thackeray's third major novel often articulated their memory of reading more than the reading itself. The process of reading, the activity of the wandering viewpoint in the middle of the text, is more prominent in Victorians' ongoing responses to installment texts, elements of which I have tried to specify in the first three chapters of this book and to which I will add in the final two chapters. In the reviews of *Esmond* cited in this chapter, however, we will see "a total view of that journey" formulated after it is over more than a dialectic between author and audience going forward as the work itself advances.

This three-volume format, which inspired a consistent vision of the whole more readily than Thackeray's serial texts, thus seemed to answer Victorian critics who wanted more cohesive structures from novelists of the age. Reviewers in Thackeray's time and since have generally agreed with Trollope that this work is "a whole from beginning to end."[3] The first-person narrator, of course, contributed to the tighter structure of *Esmond* after the discursive omniscient narrators of his earlier works. *Esmond*'s aesthetic unity was balanced, however, by limits to the readers' participation in the more open, ongoing form that characterized Thackeray's earlier serial works. As Samuel Phillips complained in the *Times* on 22 December 1852, *Esmond* seemed not to have allowed readers to become active in the story: "We desire to see a complete novel from [Thackeray's] pen, but he must give himself an unencumbered field and allow the reader as well as himself fair play."[4] The fact that Thackeray left for a speaking tour in America almost immediately after the release of the three-volume edition seemed to underscore for at least one reader the text's autonomous identity: George

81

Brimley wrote in the *Spectator* (6 November 1852) that "Mr. Thackeray has left this delightful book behind him to console London for his absence in America."[5]

From such a perspective, looking at the whole work as a single complete entity (as opposed to a series of monthly presentations from an author surrounded by periods of commentary and discussion), Thackeray's audience tended to gather together the elements of *Esmond* into a single, cohesive reading more consciously than they did his earlier, serial works. Dudley Flamm points out that the early reviews of the novel focused "on the family affairs of the Castlewoods and the love triangle of Esmond, Beatrix, and Lady Castlewood [which] led these critics to regard the ménage as not only disreputable but depraved."[6] In addition to this intense reaction to love relationships in the novel, Victorian readers also responded strongly to the subject of family history. In the same November 1852 *Spectator* George Brimley wrote: "Unity [in *Esmond*] is not given by a consecutive and self-developing story, but by the ordinary events of life blended with those peculiar to a stirring time acting on a family group, and bringing out and ripening their qualities; these again controlling the subsequent events, just as happens in life."[7] Dudley Flamm notes that *Esmond* was "a departure from Thackeray's previous work in that it was a chronicle of one family. . . ."[8] American readers of the time, in fact, were put off by what they, as the New World deliberately less obsessed with pedigree, considered an excessive concern with genealogy. The *United States Review* for March 1853 complained that "The tale abounds in genealogical descriptions, for Mr. Thackeray never mentions any individual without also acquainting you with the history of his father and his grandfather."[9] This interest in the relationship of family and history, however, organized the material of the novel for the more traditional British readers. It became a core of consistency-building.

By examining Thackeray's technique in presenting the theme of family history in *Henry Esmond* we can explore the kind of reading inspired by a three-volume work as opposed to installment novels, consistency-building more than the activity of the wandering view-point. Thackeray constructed the family history of his central character Henry Esmond in the pages of his fiction; and Victorian readers organized their experience of the novel by building for themselves an imagined House of Esmond. The reader's family tree, however, was constructed within the single basic reading inspired by a three-volume format, without the fixed places for continuing evaluation or interpretation inherent in the serial mode. That is, the tree came into being more as a whole unit than through a process that, sustained over many months, included interruptions during which readers extended or resisted key elements of the story. In a serial experience, the tracing of a family history would have been affected by the readers' own ongoing history. While *Esmond's* portrait of one family's past did create a lasting impression on the audience's mind, the sense of the fictional characters' slowly developing story was not augmented by the passing of generations in the real world. In order to identify places where the readers' world did *not* affect the novel's, we must first review in some detail the two important family histories within the fictional world.

The climactic final scene of *Henry Esmond* is the hero's repudiation of James Stuart the Pretender, that unworthy aspirant to the British throne. With his young cousin Frank at his side, Henry Esmond lists the acts of loyalty their ancestors have performed for the Stuart family and then rejects the Esmond tradition of allegiance to that royal house:

> "You will please, sir, to remember," he continued, "that our family hath ruined itself by fidelity to yours: that my grandfather spent his estate, and gave his blood and his son to die for your service; that my dear lord's grandfather (for lord you are now, Frank, by right and title too) died for the same cause; that my poor kinswoman, my father's second wife [Isabella Esmond], after giving away her honour to your wicked perjured race, sent all her wealth to the King; and got in return that precious title that lies in ashes, and this inestimable yard of blue riband. I lay this at your feet and stamp upon it: I draw this sword,

83

and break it and deny you; and had you completed the wrong you designed us [the seduction of Frank's sister, Beatrix], by heaven I would have driven it through your heart, and no more pardoned you than your father pardoned Monmouth."[10]

So articulate, so emotionally charged, so persuasive is Esmond's final dismissal of Old World values—principally those deriving from the feudal institution of aristocracy—that readers too tend to dismiss them, particularly since history has confirmed for the modern and Victorian audience the wisdom of Esmond's decision. While Thackeray's art encourages us to respond favorably to the hero's championing of democratic principles at the end of the novel, we must remember as well that to pursue his new beliefs Henry must leave England, a country where the forces of aristocracy linger in the mid-Victorian era.[11] A study of genealogy in *Henry Esmond*—and of Isabella Esmond, whose position in the Esmond family history is particularly revealing—reminds us of the force of the feudal social order in the world of Thackeray's fiction and reinforces the suspicion that Henry's subsequent life in the New World will not be entirely free from the forces that corrupted the old.[12]

During the time of *Esmond*'s composition, Thackeray was steeped in the historical period of its setting, having just prepared the lectures on English humorists of the eighteenth century delivered in London from May to July 1851. Making use of his English audience's familiarity with their own national history, he shaped basic responses to his fiction encouraging consistency-building. Thackeray and his audience knew that underlying political events in England during the last decades of the seventeenth and first decades of the eighteenth centuries were the facts of the country's then most significant genealogy—the Stuarts'. Beginning in 1649 with the execution of Britain's second Stuart monarch, Charles I, England took a series of irrevocable steps toward parliamentarian as opposed to monarchical rule that culminated in the Glorious Revolution of 1688. After the failure of Puritan rule under Cromwell in the Commonwealth years (1649–60), the Stuart Charles II returned to reign as a weak monarch in the Restoration period. His brother,

James II, succeeded him in 1685 and promptly angered Parliament by his autocratic rule and the country at large by his Catholic sympathies. In 1688 the country settled a largely ceremonial throne on the House of Orange (William III and Mary), awarding the real power of government to Parliament. James II was forced to flee the country, but throughout the reigns of Prince William and his successor, Queen Anne, English Jacobites, like the Esmonds, pursued a futile hope of returning James Stuart—and later his son, James called the Pretender—to the throne of England.

To such citizens of the future as Thackeray's readers and ourselves the fate of such Royalist sympathies is, of course, much clearer than it was to the people caught up in an age of transition, and this knowledge encourages consistency-building in the readers' evaluation of individual characters and events. No character of the novel knows, for instance, as fully as the readers do, the future of Castlewood, the Esmond family home, which is an emblem of the family's relationship to the forces of history:

> The Hall of Castlewood was built with two courts, whereof one only, the fountain court, was now inhabited, the other having been battered down in the Cromwelliam wars. In the fountain court, still in good repair, was the great hall, near to the kitchen and butteries. A dozen of living-rooms looking to the north, and communicating with the little chapel that faced eastwards and the buildings stretching from that to the main gate, and with the hall (which looked to the west) into the court now dismantled. This court had been the most magnificent of the two, until the Protector's cannon tore down one side of it before the place was taken and stormed. The besiegers entered at the terrace under the clock-tower, slaying every man of the garrison, and at their head, my lord's brother, Francis Esmond. (Pp. 27–28)

Even Henry Esmond, writing before the American Revolution (an extension of the English retreat from monarchy), is less fully aware of the ultimate fate that awaits his Royalist family than are the readers of his memoirs. Thackeray's readers discover in the course of the novel that each Esmond who tries to return the family to security and wealth enjoyed by his ancestors, instead of seeking a

85

new role for the family in a changing society, adds his own demise to the general fall of the House of Esmond. No specific deed marks the Esmond family for destruction in the way that the House of Atreus is doomed in Greek myth, but the Esmonds' reactionary worship of the Stuart monarchy makes of their genealogy a series of unhappy heirs.

This family destiny becomes a major component of the novel's meaning generated by the audience's consistency-building. Because Thackeray's text has no formal interruptions, however, as a serial does, this family doom is an especially fixed and unchanging one. The House of Esmond built by Victorian readers exhibited a clear shape in part because they had less time to speculate about individual events in the family's past than a serial audience would have before coming to the novel's conclusion, where the full pattern of history was visible. Not only were there no specific pauses in the text between parts for audiences to project their own concerns via a wandering viewpoint, but the shortened time of reading from the usual nineteen-month serial experience did not encourage the readers' sense of time's passing in life to extend the fiction's continuing history. To see more precisely how the readers' time spent in pursuing the fictional family history *might* have affected the literary experience, however, we must consider first the facts of the Esmond genealogy.

In Thackeray's fiction the Esmond family tree begins with Edward, earl and marquis of Esmond (see family tree).[13] Since he had no male heir, the marquisate passed out of the family at his death. His only daughter, Dorothea, married Henry Poyns, a page in her father's house. Francis, the son and heir of Dorothea and Henry, retained the maternal name of Esmond, but not, of course, his grandfather's title. Many of his descendents are, in turn, obsessed with returning the Esmond name to the rank it bore in Edward's time. Their loyalty to the Stuart family during the years of the Protectorate and the Restoration is inextricably bound up with the claims to land and rank conferred on them by the royal family. Sir George Esmond "incurred both expense and danger" (p. 11) in

86

The House of Esmond

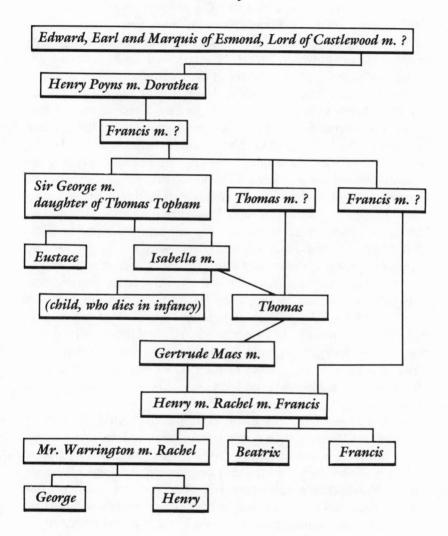

87

James I's behalf during that monarch's German campaigns; in return he was named the first Lord Castlewood in 1643. Francis's third eldest son (also a Francis) and George's son (Eustace) were killed fighting against the Commonwealth. None of these aspirants to Stuart favor, however, excels the fervor of Isabella Esmond, Sir George's daughter, in her pursuit of the marquisate.

In developing the character of Isabella Esmond, Thackeray relies on his audience's familiarity with the cast of characters that had peopled his earlier fiction, on class stereotypes, and on the practice of pairing characters (Becky Sharp and Amelia Sedley, Blanche Amory and Laura Pendennis) whose complementary fates help structure a work of art. Samuel Phillips noted in the *Times* on 22 December 1852 that "All our friends that entertained us for so many months in *Vanity Fair* and *Pendennis* have their *facsimiles* in Mr. Esmond's volume."[14] Isabella has ancestors in characters like Lady Bareacres and Lady Clavering. Isabella is also, as George Brimley observed at the novel's first appearance, a type, a "dowager Viscountess [who] is a more faithful than flattering portrait of a class of ladies of rank of that time."[15] And comparisons between Isabella and Rachel Esmond, as potential sponsors of the illegitimate Henry Esmond and as matriarchs of the House of Esmond, provide an important organizing principle for readers of the novel. Linking the contrasting values of the two women to the course of their own national history, the Victorian audience created a picture of the past.

This picture of Isabella Esmond, however, tended to be more static and unchanging than it might have been had the text insisted on month-long pauses in the reading in which alternative versions of family events might have been entertained for longer periods within the wandering viewpoint. Isabella's character and her influence on the novel's causality might have been further developed by the reader in the space between numbers, as happened with Amelia Sedley in *Vanity Fair*. And the audience's identification with some of Isabella's traits and beliefs might have been deepened, even to the point of challenging more substantially the reader's ideas about themselves, had the consequences of her actions not been revealed so promptly. Instead, the portrait of Isabella built up in the course of reading the three-volume novel firmly establishes her identity and her role in the Esmond family history. Thackeray's portrait of Isabella and her place in the Esmond genealogy is recognized by the reader's consistency-building as a finished definition of Old World loyalty to the king.

Thackeray's original readers learned in the course of the novel that the daughter of the second Lord Castlewood, Isabella, made good use of her place at court before the story's hero came into the world: she became the mistress of the future James II, then the duke of York. Lady Castlewood recounts her last interview with that monarch, then in exile, to her young page, Henry Esmond: "'Perhaps he remembered old times, when Isabella Esmond was young and fair; perhaps he recalled the day when 'twas not I that knelt—at least he spoke to me with a voice that reminded me of days gone by" (p. 44).[16] At that time of her youth, Isabella had grand plans for her branch of the Esmond family: she hoped to graft it to the royal tree, that other significantly causal genealogy of the novel. Isabella is reminded of that intention in a famous scene of court intrigue when Lady Marlborough, Jack Churchill's wife, rebuffs her petition for Henry Esmond's advancement. Jack's sister is the mother of the duke of Berwick, the bastard son of James II, who has received favors from Lady Marlborough. Isabella complains to her court rival that the Churchills' illegitimate son has been unfairly promoted while the Esmonds' (that is, Henry) has been ignored: "'Madam,' says the Duchess, 'you know whose fault it is that there are no such dukes in the Esmond family too, and how that little scheme of a certain lady miscarried'" (p. 254). Isabella's unreasonable belief in her fertility—as Lady Castlewood, past the age of forty, she is "constantly sending over to Hexton for the doctor, and announcing to her friends the arrival of an heir" (p. 16)—may even suggest that only an inability to conceive a child by James prevented her from uniting the Esmond line with the Stuart. Isabella's pursuit of James is determined in part by the family's past; the desire to

89

return the Esmond name and fortune to its original status lies behind the loyalties and actions of preceding Esmond generations and becomes her heritage.

Although her desire to bear a child by James is not fulfilled, her influence at court, she believes, can still be used to forge an appropriate future for her family. Isabella counts on profiting from the traditional system of royal patronage. Unfortunately for her, that system is beginning to give way in James's time to the modern principle of promotion by merit. Isabella accepts the suit of her cousin, Frank Esmond, though he is "her junior by several years" (p. 13), because she feels she can maneuver, through her influence at court, a younger, less sophisticated partner toward a future of her own designing. Frank, however, both surprises and insults his wealthy, influential cousin: "having paid his court, and being admitted to the intimacy of the house, he suddenly flung up his suit, when it seemed to be pretty prosperous, without giving a pretext for his behavior" (p. 13). It is Frank's discovery of Isabella's relationship with the king that explodes their romance: "he left the Court and went to Tangier in a rage at discovering that his promotion depended on the complaisance of his elderly affianced bride" (p. 13). Displaying an unconscious sensitivity to a trend of the future, a belief in meritocracy, Frank explains to his friend, Jack Churchill: "'Jack, your sister may be so-and-so, but by Jove my wife sha'n't!' . . . Few men were so jealous about the point of honour in those days; and gentlemen of good birth and lineage thought a royal blot was an ornament to their family coat" (p. 13). This unwillingness to accept the prerogatives of a corrupt monarchy foreshadows Frank's later allegiance to Prince William and his repudiation of the traditional Esmond loyalties. He arrives, on the strength of his feelings, at a position that the more intellectual Henry achieves only after many years of senseless devotion to the Stuart cause.

Although she fails to realize her alliance with the youngest branch of Esmonds, Isabella finally makes an even more profitable marriage with her other cousin, Thomas Esmond, heir to Lord Castlewood, her father. This match also seems suited to her attempt

90

to return the family to its former glory, since Thomas, who "as truth must be told, was no better than a hanger-on of ordinaries" (p. 14), shows his willingness to be led by marrying a cousin "now of more than middle age" (p. 14). This union also returns the one independent branch of the Esmond family to the Tory cause. Thomas's father had been estranged from the head of the house, Sir George Esmond, since he joined the usurper's party. In accepting this change of national character, the elder Thomas had freed himself from the family curse, a blind loyalty to the Stuarts. When the younger Thomas marries Isabella, however, he allies his father's branch of the Esmonds again to its doomed cause.

Before his submission to the family fate, however, the younger Thomas had added another branch to the family tree whose existence threatens the future envisioned by Isabella. Although Lady Castlewood does not learn of it until three years later, Thomas was actually married to Gertrude Maes at the time he was courting his cousin Isabella. Thomas and Gertrude's son, of course, is Henry Esmond—technically the legal heir of the house and the only Esmond not born under the curse of Tory loyalty. When Isabella learns of his paternity, she immediately brings him to Castlewood and, with Father Holt's assistance, begins the boy's education in her own philosophy (pp. 347–48). Isabella's decision to conceal Henry's legitimacy proves a fatal error to her own ambition. Unable to offer any public justification for keeping Henry under her control, she allows him to stay at Castlewood after her own arrest and imprisonment at Hexam (pp. 347–48). The new Lady Castlewood, Rachel Esmond, thus becomes a rival influence to Isabella in the determination of Henry's fate and of the future course of the entire Esmond family.

That rivalry, then, is a major theme in Henry's autobiography which inspires, through consistency-building, a shape to the readers' experience: Rachel's pious, Anglican domesticity is contrasted with the worldly, Catholic Isabella's obsession to retain the social preeminence the Esmonds had enjoyed in Edward's time.[17] What Thackeray's readers learned about Isabella's motives from the Esmond genealogy expands their understanding of the Isabella Henry

91

remembers, the Isabella seen from Henry's limited point of view. The older Henry Esmond, composing in his Virginia retirement some forty years after the events in question, remembers the Tory viscountess as the first cause of misfortune in his life, but he admits that she "hath repaired, by subsequent kindness to him, these severeties, which it must be owned made his childhood very unhappy" (p. 32). When Esmond speaks of Isabella in his memoirs, he tends to be less severe in judging her actions than we might be, having taken a more studied look at her role in furthering the Esmond family fortune.

At times Thackeray seems to want to draw attention to the Isabella who figures prominently in the Esmond genealogy—so much so, in fact, that he breaks the monopoly of Henry's first-person narrative to emphasize Isabella's obsessive concern with the Esmond family fortunes.[18] Henry's daughter, Rachel Esmond Warrington, who writes a preface to his memoirs before they are published, occasionally intrudes with footnotes to Esmond's narrative. By including her point of view in the novel, Thackeray provides another source of information about the facts of Henry's life.

In one way, these footnotes serve a function similar to that of the pauses in Thackeray's installment texts, encouraging the reader not to let one version of events dominate the fictional landscape. The readers turn from the primary text (Henry's autobiography) to another narrative (Rachel's commentary) just as, in a serial text, they moved via a wandering viewpoint between the novel's world and their own, sometimes interpreting one on the basis of their experience in the other. Thackeray's readers, for instance, had applied to his characters Warrington and Pendennis professional standards articulated in the contemporary debate about the nature and value of literary effort. Since the text of *Henry Esmond* continues immediately after the footnote, however, the readers resume this story without pause. They modify their understanding of family history according to the information provided by Rachel Esmond Warrington but are not encouraged to let their personal concerns, their own history, mingle with and alter the novel's history. The portrait of Isabella is completed in this three-volume text without prolonged speculation about her character by the reader, even though more than one narrator reports on her life.

In one footnote to her father's text Rachel makes the central observation that Isabella was obsessed with the desire to regain the rank of marquis for her family:

> To have this rank of Marquis restored in the family had always been my Lady Viscountess's ambition; and her old maiden aunt, Barbara Topham, the goldsmith's daughter, dying about this time, and leaving all her property to Lady Castlewood, I have heard that her ladyship sent almost the whole of the money to King James, a proceeding which so irritated my Lord Castlewood that he actually went to the parish church, and was only appeased by the Marquis's title which his exiled Majesty sent to him in return for the £15,000 his faithful subject lent him. (P. 54)

This is the most direct statement in the novel of Isabella's motives; coming as it does in a footnote to Esmond's text, it suggests that Henry himself never realized the reasons behind much of his stepmother's behavior. In denying his heritage to begin a new life in the New World, Esmond is, as a matter of principle, less concerned with such Old World history: "we two [Henry and Rachel] cared no longer to live in England: and Frank formally and joyfully yielded over to us the possession of that estate which we now occupy, far away from Europe and its troubles . . ." (p. 493). His daughter Rachel, however, who "own[s] to *a decent respect* for my name" (p. xli), has proudly studied the Esmond genealogy in detail and probably blames Isabella for the fact that she herself is not the daughter of a marquis. Granting as little importance to the Esmond family history as he does to his own right to the title of Lord Castlewood, Esmond is less critical of Isabella as he writes his autobiography than is his daughter when she edits those memoirs.

In Henry's writings, Isabella at first appears a frightening creature indeed, especially in opposition to the other important older woman in his life, Rachel Esmond. Thackeray's practice of contrasting these two figures underscores the novel's important theme of

93

family history. So moving is the protagonist's first meeting with Rachel that it precedes in his memoirs, though not in history, his introduction to Isabella:

> "My name is Henry Esmond," said the lad, looking up at her in a sort of delight and wonder, for she had come upon him as a *Dea certè*, and appeared the most charming object he had ever looked on. Her golden hair was shining in the gold of the sun; her complexion was of a dazzling bloom; her lips smiling, and her eyes beaming with a kindness which made Harry Esmond's heart to beat with surprise. (P. 5)

Against such a vision of seemingly divine goodness the elder viscountess's initial appearance is all the more frightening in Henry's description:

> My Lady Viscountess's face was daubed with white and red up to the eyes, to which the paint gave an unearthly glare; she had a tower of lace on her head, under which was a bush of black curls—borrowed curls—so that no wonder little Harry Esmond was scared when he was first presented to her—the kind priest acting as master of the ceremonies at that solemn introduction—and he stared at her with eyes almost as great as her own, as he had stared at the player-woman who acted the wicked tragedy-queen, when the players came down to Ealing Fair. (Pp. 24–25)

Although the almost point-for-point comparison—of hair, eyes, complexion—insists on Isabella's artificiality, Henry, having reconciled himself since this scene to her faults, is being more than fair to the Lady Viscountess; he does not link her falseness with any palpable betrayal of important values but with the exaggerated display of the theater. It is an awareness of Isabella's complicity in the Esmond family's political ambitions, of the pattern of the Esmond genealogy, which reminds Thackeray's readers of the extent of her betrayal of such values as honesty, affection, and integrity.

From the point at which Isabella is made a captive at Hexam Castle by King William, Henry is passionately devoted to another

Esmond, Rachel, who assumes her rival's place as mistress of Castlewood. Isabella's role in Henry's future, however, is not ended; whenever the intensity of Henry and Rachel's affection causes a break in their relationship, she becomes—as the inspiration of his Tory sympathies—an important and dangerous influence in the shaping of Esmond's destiny. The two opposing types, Rachel and Isabella, are rivals not only for Henry's affection but also for the loyalties of the next legitimate Esmond generation, Frank and Beatrix. Frank's marriage to the daughter of a German count is hardly a victory for Rachel; falling under the influence of Father Holt, Frank takes Henry's place in religious and political (as well as legal) terms as the male heir of Isabella's Tory and Catholic sympathies (p. 344). And Beatrix, as I shall show presently, becomes for Isabella a perfect protégée. Only to Henry does Rachel successfully pass on her values, though he too seems for a time to have become a disciple of Isabella.

The playing out of these next stages in the Esmond destiny is Thackeray's further exposition of the central theme, an individual family's relationship to history. From their perspective in the mid-nineteenth century, Thackeray's Victorian readers continued their assessment of the past and its relationship to the present by comparing Rachel's and Isabella's strategies in securing stability for the family. This consistency-building goes on, however, primarily as the novel is being read, in the single block of time when the Victorian audience is building its House of Esmond, because Rachel's success and Isabella's failure are made clear by the novel's end. The family history's clear delineation is less affected by the individual and collective readers' concerns than would have been the case had there been formal interruptions in the text, fixed delays in the reading process that would have encouraged speculation via the wandering viewpoint about specific points, particularly issues raised just before enforced pauses in reading. In the three-volume reading experience, the text establishes more clearly for its audience the terms of its own interpretation—in this case, Rachel and Isabella as alternative choices for the Esmond future.

95

Although Isabella appears to have lost out fairly early in the battle for loyalty from younger members of the family, she continues to influence indirectly the course of history. Rachel marries the man who had rejected Isabella and wins Henry's devotion while Thomas's wife was a prisoner at Hexam Castle. When the young Henry Esmond first leaves Castlewood, though, to go to Cambridge, he visits Isabella at Chelsea. Not insensitive to this opportunity for regaining Henry's affection, the dowager "bade Mr. Esmond not to forget to pay her a visit whenever he passed through London, and carried her graciousness so far as to send a purse with twenty guineas for him, to the tavern at which my lord put up (the 'Greyhound,' in Charing Cross); and, along with this welcome gift for her kinsman, she sent a little doll for a present to my lord's little daughter Beatrix, who was growing beyond the age of dolls by this time, and was as tall almost as her venerable relative" (p. 105). Before long, the dowager Esmond makes her donation to Henry's college expenses an annual event, and Henry thereafter spends his Christmases at Chelsea (p. 108). When, at her husband's death, Rachel vows that she will never see Henry again, Isabella writes to him in her "strange barbarous French": *"Quand vous seray hor prison venay me voyre. J'auray soing de vous. Si cette petite Prude veut se défaire de song pety Monste (Hélas je craing qùil ne soy trotar!) je m'en chargeray. J'ay encor quelqu interay et quelques escus de costay"* (p. 186). When Henry does accept the offer to stay near her, she loses no time in continuing the education she and Father Holt had begun in his early childhood. "She introduced him to her company, of which she entertained a good deal—of the adherents of King James of course—and a great deal of loud intriguing took place over her card-tables. She presented Mr. Esmond as her kinsman to many persons of honour; she supplied him not illiberally with money, which he had no scruple in accepting from her, considering the relationship which he bore to her, and the sacrifices which he himself was making in behalf of the family" (p. 192). Having been betrayed once, he believes, in his affection for Rachel, however, Esmond "made up his mind to continue at no woman's apronstrings longer . . ." (p. 102). Joining the military, he wisely avoids further association with his stepmother's society. The Tory acquaintances he makes at Chelsea, however—in addition to his early training in his cousin's intrigues—provide the foundation for his most wrongheaded action of the novel, the plot to bring the Pretender to England. Although he initiates that scheme specifically to impress and win Beatrix, Isabella's influence on the course of his life is clear in the mechanics and materials with which he carries out the venture.

Thackeray's emphasis on the force of family history also leads his readers to understand that Isabella's effect on Henry's life is continued through Beatrix, for Beatrix is Isabella's spiritual if not her legal heir.[19] Isabella had long styled herself as Diana, the virgin huntress, in which pose she appears in the Esmond family gallery at Castlewood: "My Lady Dowager had left off this particular habit of huntress when she married. But though she was now considerably past sixty years of age, I believe she thought that airy nymph could still be easily recognized in the venerable personage who gave an audience to Harry . . ." (p. 104). Returning from his third year at Cambridge, Henry finds in Beatrix "a mien and shape haughty and beautiful, such as that of the famous antique statue of the huntress Diana—at one time haughty, rapid, imperious, with eyes and arrows that dart and kill" (p. 133). Isabella sees in Beatrix, "a child of great beauty and many winning ways" (p. 61), a possible successor to her role as architect of the family's future. Beatrix herself wonders how Rachel "should have had such a child" (p. 420) as herself; she is in behavior and attitude so much more akin to the worldly Viscountess Esmond than the domestic and pious Rachel Esmond. Isabella uses her influence with Lady Marlborough to advance her protégée at court, where the latter finds no want of admirers; and, as Isabella's political heir apparent—Beatrix is "as frantic about the King as her elderly kinswoman" (p. 331)—she inspires Esmond's service in the Pretender's cause. When Henry, Rachel, and Beatrix prepare Castlewood for the clandestine arrival of the Pretender late in the novel, Beatrix inherits "Viscountess Isabel's sleeping apartment . . . where Esmond perfectly well remembered seeing the old lady sitting up in the bed, in her night-rail, that morning when the

97

troop of guard came to fetch her" (p. 418). As Henry learns later to his own cost, Beatrix is eager to repeat her relative's earlier dramatic pose of total allegiance to the Stuart will.

Although Isabella dies while Henry is trying to win Beatrix, Thackeray stresses her continuing influence on the Esmond family history through the inheritance she leaves the novel's protagonist. Isabella provides her "adopted son" (p. 319) a small fortune, enough to make Henry, "if not rich, at least easy for life" (p. 333). The dowager also leaves Henry her "Royal jewels of great value" (p. 14), apparently a gift from James II. These diamonds become a symbol of the family curse, the Esmonds' tie to the Stuarts, appearing significantly at moments of Henry's near submission to the family fate. Thackeray's audience is thus reminded of the danger of a blind allegiance to one family and one course in history.

Henry's original intention is to give the diamonds to Beatrix when he has finally won her love. However, she accepts the suit of another Jacobite, and an important minister in Queen Anne's court, the duke of Hamilton. Sadly but magnanimously Henry presents "the diamonds my father's widow left me" to the future duchess: "and the next minute the necklace was where Belinda's cross is in Mr. Pope's admirable poem, and glittering on the whitest and most pretty-shaped neck in all England" (pp. 385–86). Had the Duke survived, Henry—free of the diamonds—would also have been free of the family curse. After Hamilton's untimely death, however, Beatrix returns the diamonds, declaring to Esmond her renunciation of worldly success:

> Here stood Beatrix in her black robes, holding a box in her hand; 'twas that which Esmond had given her before her marriage, stamped with a coronet which the disappointed girl was never to wear; and containing his aunt's legacy of diamonds.
> "You had best take these with you, Harry," says she; "I have no need of diamonds any more." (P. 418)

His desire to possess Beatrix thus rekindled, Henry asks her not to refuse him or the jewels at that moment: "Never shake your head, but hear me; say you will hear me a year hence. If I come back to you and bring you fame, will that please you" (p. 419). Beatrix hints that should Henry succeed in bringing the Pretender to England she may yet give him her heart. Serving the Stuart cause to win this heartless creature, however, would be both evidence of the family curse and the terms of its fulfillment. Henry is saved from this family doom as much by demonstrations of vice in others as by urgings of virtue in himself.

Thackeray completes his exploration of the theme of family loyalties through the climactic scene in which Henry rejects the Esmond tradition of blind allegiance to the Stuarts. His Victorian audience can see the link to its own parliamentarian age in this resolution of the novel's plot. Such consistency-building, of course, comes more quickly to *Esmond* than to Thackeray's two earlier novels, whose ends take more than eighteen months to arrive. Some of the questions readers may have entertained—about Isabella and the history of the House of Esmond—are answered or forgotten for readers who learn so quickly where this story leads. And Henry himself convincingly articulates the lessons of that history in the novel's famous concluding scenes.

Henry finally renounces his love for Beatrix when he sees in her flirtation with the Pretender, and in James's pursuit of her, a total denial of the principles that had directed him in his attempts to serve the Stuarts. He thus escapes the family curse by rejecting—in the form of its agent, Beatrix—Isabella's legacy, the Esmond obsession with rank, and by denying as well both the symbol and the embodiment of the Tory cause, James himself. The diamonds, appropriately worn by Beatrix on the day of the Pretender's arrival at Castlewood, are returned to Esmond when he banishes her from the royal presence: "I have brought back," says she "to the Marquis of Esmond the present he deigned to make me in days when he trusted me better than now. I will never accept a benefit or a kindness from Henry Esmond more, and I give back these family diamonds, which belonged to one king's mistress, to the gentleman that suspected I should be another" (p. 461).

In this venomous speech Beatrix is at least accurate in her accusations: the "family" diamonds logically belong with the "Marquis of Esmond," not to Henry Esmond, who eschews both family

99

wealth and title; she will have nothing further to do with "Henry Esmond," the man who chooses not to pursue the worldly values she worships. Isabella was a king's mistress who does not deserve Esmond's respect; and Beatrix would have been another, as she subsequently proves. Beatrix's mother, Rachel, demonstrates an allegiance to the proper values of the novel and of the Henry Esmond who retires to Virginia. On the last page of his memoirs Henry fondly recalls: "the only jewel by which my wife sets any store, and from which she had never parted, is that gold button she took from my arm on the day when she visited me in prison, and which she wore ever after as she told me, on the tenderest heart in the world" (p. 493).

Thackeray's readers conclude, then, that Isabella's desire to direct the Esmond future through Henry and her young Diana ends in disappointment, for Beatrix loses both the duke of Hamilton and the Pretender, and Henry renounces his allegiance to the Stuarts, which was to have returned the marquisate to the family. Guided by Isabella's philosophy and example, Beatrix had pursued the highest rank and wealth of the kingdom, and it led to the fulfillment of the family curse: "ever after that day at Castlewood, when we rescued her, she persisted in holding all her family as her enemies, and left us, and escaped to France, to what a fate I disdain to tell" (p. 492). Her brother's fate is no more promising for the Esmond future: "weak, as perhaps all our race hath been, and led by women," Frank "had been made to marry the whole of that German family with whom he had connected himself" (p. 492). Henry, in renouncing Isabella's ethics, escapes the family curse to a new beginning in a new world: he tells Beatrix, "I am not quite clever enough, or not rogue enough—I know not which—for the Old World. I may make a place for myself in the New, which is not so full; and found a family there" (pp. 376–77).

The family that Henry and Rachel found in Virginia does seem to be endorsed by Thackeray's completed novel.[20] The English House of Esmond—as Rachel once described it, "an old dull house, half-ruined, and the rest only half-furnished" (p. 101)—has lost its prestige and its power under Isabella's direction. Esmond's final realization of the nature of the curse on his house manifests itself in the dramatic denial of his birthright (as the Pretender and Frank Esmond look on, he burns the papers naming him rightful heir to Thomas Esmond) and in his eloquent repudiation of the Esmond allegiance to James Stuart, "whose race seemed to be doomed like the Atridae of old" (p. 423). Telling Frank about Father Holt's secret window-entrance to Castlewood in that same dramatic scene, Esmond also debunks any glorified version of his own family history: "the foundress of our family [Dorothea Esmond] let our ancestor [Henry Poyns] in in that way" (p. 484). Rachel, the elder viscountess's rival throughout much of Henry's lifetime, becomes in the end the unchallenged mistress of the real Esmond future. And Henry appears for this moment as the true heir, legally and spiritually, of a once noble family, just as George I, Henry finally admits, is the rightful heir to the English throne.[21] Isabella's life runs out, ironically, while she is playing at cards when she would have been plotting with kings—Henry remembers her last words, appropriately, as "Tierce to a King" (p. 333). Henry and Rachel leave England engaged in the more serious occupation they have inherited from her—rebuilding in America the House of Esmond.[22]

Of course, Thackeray has included in the text of *Henry Esmond* one additional source of information besides the first-person narrator, and Rachel Esmond Warrington's voice of the future (that is, whatever comes after Henry's life) exudes that same excessive pride in her lineage that characterized her step-grandmother, Isabella Esmond, and her half-sister, Beatrix Esmond. Thus, Victorian readers are reminded that the Old World Esmond character does not die out, that some part of it travels to America with Henry and Rachel as well as continuing at home in England. Henry's decision to leave his country seems the best alternative open to him, given his personal and historical circumstances. As he himself observes at one point, "In England you can but belong to one party or t'other, and you take the house you live in with all its encumbrances, its retainers, its antique discomforts, and ruins even; you patch up, but you never build up anew" (p. 393). The novel's final message seems to be that the House of Esmond cound never really be rebuilt entirely anew in England or America.

As Thackeray's readers took in this three-volume production in 1852, they too pieced together a family history, building up in their imaginations a House of Esmond with its lessons about family identity, personal loyalty, and social history. That this experience was more self-contained and focused than those inspired by his earlier works is a product in part of its different publication format. After July 1853 discussion of *Esmond* (published October 1852) was generally limited to references in reviews of Thackeray's work as a whole and to discussions of contemporary fiction, whereas both his earlier works were on the public mind for essentially two years as additional installments continued to be issued. Victorian readers, then, were building the House of Esmond primarily for the few weeks it took to read those three volumes. Within that (comparatively) short time, fictional generations came and went more quickly than they did with *Pendennis,* for instance, in which Arthur replaces his uncle as the family patriarch over a two-year span in readers' lives. The audience's experience of history's slow unfolding—the distance from Edward, earl and marquis of Esmond, to Rachel Esmond Warrington—is lessened in this sense with *Esmond,* although not, of course, without other gains in artistic effect already well documented in Thackeray criticism. Further, no formal opportunities—gaps in the text—are provided Thackeray's audience for evaluation or revision, before the fiction is concluded and the lessons of history are realized. Characters are more fixed in individual identity and in telling contrasts by a text that omits the places in earlier novels where the audiences had interjected their own concerns. The final portrait is, of course, a memorable one; but the manner of reading *Henry Esmond* significantly shaped its identity for the Victorian audience.

Choosing another family history as the subject for his next novel, *The Newcomes,* Thackeray returned to the serial format. Underscoring this novel's sense of time's passing through the monthly issue of installments, Thackeray regained special means to an intense and continuing influence on the consciousness of his age.

Although consistency-building continues in what some have considered his masterpiece, it is Thackeray's textual representation of the wandering viewpoint in a serial experience that needs exploration here.

5
Old Stories in *The Newcomes*

Thackeray's lingering farewell at the end of *The Newcomes* (1853–55) reminds us of the strength of the Victorian serial novelist's relationship with his reader—always threatened with parting (the end of the monthly number), but consoled that they are soon to meet again:

> My belief then is, that in Fable-land somewhere Ethel and Clive are living most comfortably together. . . . But for you, dear friend [the reader], it is as you like. You may settle your Fable-land in your own fashion. Anything you like happens in Fable-land. . . . Ah, happy, harmlesss, Fable-land, where these things are! Friendly reader! may you and the author meet there on some future day! He hopes so; as he yet keeps a lingering hold of your hand, and bids you farewell with a kind heart.[1]

Warmed by the twenty-three months of sharing this fictional world—the "Fable-land" where Ethel and Clive Newcome, Arthur and Laura Pendennis, and all the others have existed—Thackeray holds on to the reader's hand with a melancholy intensity that not only offers a clue to the structure of this long and frequently under-rated novel,[2] but also provides a glimpse into the dynamics of reading a serially published novel in Victorian England. In this text the rhythm of serial reading—meetings and partings—is intimately connected to theme.

Much has already been written about the care with which the great nineteenth-century novelists like Thackeray constructed works of traditional three-volume length in thirty-two-page parts, monthly installments that could stand individually almost as short stories yet fit together in the end into a complete whole. The classic study of Victorian novel composition is, of course, John Butt and Kathleen Tillotson's *Dickens at Work* (London: Methuen, 1957), which has been followed by J. A. Sutherland's *Thackeray at Work* (London: Athlone Press, 1974). Edgar Harden, who has been particularly interested in the composition of *The Newcomes,* provides a typical justification for this kind of study: "We need to understand in considerable detail the evolution of Thackeray's novels through different manuscript stages to their appearance in serial format, for only such knowledge can help us in the case of such novels as *The Newcomes* to perceive the realities of shaping serial fiction into equal monthly parts, and the qualities of the novelists' creative genius that were challenged and called forth by such realities."[3] I am here, however, more interested in the effect on the readers of those carefully constructed parts, in the qualities of their imagination "challenged and called forth by such realities," in the rhythm of reading Thackeray.

The regular pace of serial novel reading and its relation to the Victorian frame of mind are phenomena little analyzed by modern scholars, in part because of post-James assumptions about the structure of fiction. Most of these modern critical constructs are primarily spatial in nature and do not favor the kind of temporal framework most helpful in explaining literary experiences of long, midcentury novels like *The Newcomes*. In fact, when James himself (in his preface to *The Tragic Muse*) referred to *The Newcomes* (and by implication much long Victorian fiction) as a "great loose baggy monster," his very terms established the framework within which the novel was to be found lacking.

Innovative directions in literary scholarship inspired by reader-oriented criticism. however, provide some helpful new tools for understanding the serial novel experience in Victorian England. In

her introduction to an anthology of reader-response criticism, Jane
P. Tompkins points us toward the temporal nature of reading:

> Whereas Iser chronicles broad-gauge shifts in the reader's attitude
> toward the text—his construction and reconstruction of a character or
> his emerging apprehension of a theme—Fish rivets attention on the
> sequence of decisions, revisions, anticipations, reversals, and recov-
> eries that the reader performs as he negotiates the text sentence by
> sentence and phrase by phrase. . . . Literature, as a consequence, is
> not regarded as a fixed object of attention but as a sequence of events
> that unfolds within the reader's mind.[4]

Focusing on the sequential nature of the reading experience as it is
dramatically underscored by the serial format of Victorian fiction,
this discussion of *The Newcomes* attempts to show how a work that
has stood for a weakness in the nineteenth-century novel actually
represents one of that tradition's great strengths.

Whenever the serial reader has been considered by critics, it is
usually suspense that has been identified as the primary force of his
involvement with the text.[5] But as Thackeray, a very shrewd critic
of the fiction of his day, had already discovered, such end-of-the-
number, cliff-hanging thrills are short-term, unlikely alone to sustain a great work of literature. Thackeray explains in the overture to
The Newcomes that we already know what is going to happen next in
his fourth major novel because the human comedy is essentially
changeless. All stories, he insists, are really only versions of one
story:

> What stories are new? . . . With the very first page of the human story
> do not love, and lies too, begin? . . . The sun shines to-day as he did
> when he first began shining; and the birds in the tree overhead, while
> I am writing, sing very much the same note that they have sung ever
> since they were finches. Nay, since last he besought good-natured
> friends to listen once a month to his talking, a friend of the writer has
> seen the New World, and found the (featherless) birds there exceed-
> ingly like their brethen of Europe. (1:4–5)

107

But although "all stories [are] old" (1:199), there are always listeners: "There may be nothing new under and including the sun," continues Thackeray in his overture, "but it looks fresh every morning, and we rise with it to toil, hope, scheme, laugh, struggle, love, suffer, until the night comes and quiet. And then will wake Morrow and the eyes that look on it; and so *da capo*." We want to hear this "old story" in part because we, like the characters of the novel, are living it. Thackeray's subject in *The Newcomes* includes familiar themes of Victorian literature and modern man—the middle-class "newcomer's" rise to success in an evolving democratic, capitalistic society, and his discovery that in his ascent he has lost track of essential values from the past that give fuller meaning to life. Further, Victorians enjoyed reading this particular story in the last century because its serial appearance embodied the fundamental temporal frame of reference in Victorian life.

Because what happens in a Thackeray novel is in one sense known from the beginning, the audience's experience involves, as I argued in chapter 2, not only the traditional movement forward in pursuit of plot but also an evolution of perspective, a series of changes in the position from which readers view the events of the fictional world and the context within which they fit those events. Understanding comes to characters and readers, then, through a steady assimilation of information, as well as through sudden intense moments of insight. Both processes have their analogues in *The Newcomes*'s serial form.

Perhaps the most significant event of *The Newcomes,* for instance, is the marriage of convenience, "which so many folks of the family about which this story treats are engaged in arranging" (1:334).[6] Although it is a major, recurring action of the novel, the motives and consequences of the arranged marriage are, the narrator admits, known by all of us from the start: "This ceremony amongst us is so stale and common that, to be sure, there is no need to describe its rites, and as women sell themselves for what you can call an establishment every day, to the applause of themselves, their parents, and the world, why on earth should a man ape at originality, and pretend to pity them?" (1:301). It is not only the acting

108

out of this old story that Thackeray pursues but also the alterations in the ways the narrative presents it. Even as this one passage continues, its ironic tone, increasingly apparent, fits the same known event into broader and broader contexts: "Never mind about the lies at the altar, the blasphemy against the godlike name of love, the sordid surrender, the smiling dishonour. What the deuce does a *mariage de convenance* mean but all this, and are not such sober Hymeneal torches more satisfactory often than the most brilliant love-matches that ever flamed and burnt out? Of course" (1:301–2). To reveal the extent of an ideal's corruption, the narrative enumerates the ingredients of what at first seemed merely a common travesty: the formal vows taken in vain, the hypocritical worship of traditional gods, the sorry loss of freedom linked with the pleasure of conquest, the calculated gesture replacing spontaneous honest emotion. It is this new context—the sheer breadth of betrayal—into which we fit what we already know that matters in Thackeray's fiction.

Jean Sudrann makes a similar point in her discussion of time in Thackeray, which includes the best explanation to date of the fundamental style of *The Newcomes*. She identifies the way in which specific events—Clara Pulleyn's marriage of convenience to Barnes Newcome, for instance—appear in ever-widening contexts in the narrative: "By a narrative technique of point and counterpoint, events of time present are surrounded by events of time past to picture the ever recurring and relentless sacrifice of fragile human feeling in the market place of wealth and rank."[7] In the course of the novel, the reader comes to see the destruction of Clive and Ethel's potential love in the context of many related situations past and present—the Colonel and Léonore de Blois's unrequited love, political marriages at Park Lane and Bryanstone Square, Arthur and Laura Pendennis's ideal union. The reader's movement is not only forward in time toward the end of these relationships but also out of time toward a point where all these events are encompassed in a single vision. While the final reward of this experience is the traditional discovery of where all the characters end up (the resolution of a suspenseful plot), there are also intermediate moments of inspired vision for the Thackeray reader, points in the narrative where the scope of the entire novel is suddenly glimpsed. I wish to identify such visions, fresh encounters with the one "old story," more fully here before relating them to the experience of reading serially published fiction.

The many different narrators of the novel provide one obvious device for manipulating the reader's perspective on such old stories as the marriage of convenience. Thackeray himself appears in the overture and epilogue of *The Newcomes,* establishing a detached, ironic perspective on the fates of his creations. He recalls the omniscient narrative voice Thackeray employed in *Vanity Fair,* and he generally keeps the reader at a distance from the emotional lives of the characters. Arthur Pendennis, through large parts of the novel speaking with the same distanced authorial voice, is at other moments so intimately involved with the Newcome family that his narrative loses its objectivity, even becomes sentimental as it insists the reader identify with his favorite characters. Incidental narrators of the text, like Major Pendennis and Tom Eaves, provide Arthur Pendennis with substantial, uninterrupted commentary on particular events, and thus involve the reader more directly along their own lines of interest. And the novel's many letter writers and those characters speaking in dramatic scenes unannotated by authorial commentary also involve the reader more intimately with the emotional lives of the fiction, sometimes rivaling the intensity of first-person narrative in Thackeray's *Henry Esmond.*

The use of all these narrative points of view clearly allows Thackeray to control the reader's perspective on specific events. An early report by Pendennis of the Colonel's love affair with Léonore de Blois, for example, keeps us at a safe emotional distance from the characters: "What happens when two young folks of eighteen, handsome and ardent, generous and impetuous, alone in the world, or without strong affections to bind them elsewhere,—what happens when they meet daily over French dictionaries, embroidery frames, or indeed, upon any business whatever?" (1:24). The humorous, anecdotal tone is appropriate for this early summary of past events, but a change of narrator soon forces closer identifica-

110

tion with the characters and a shifting of the context within which the reader views these events. Assessing her life since that moment, which she will later admit to Ethel Newcome has been "nearly fifty years dying" (2:102), Léonore, now Madame de Florac, writes to the Colonel after "many years of absence, of silence": "My friend, I hope there was not that difference of age between your wife and you that I have known in other unions [i.e., her own]. . . . As I write the past comes back to me. I see a noble young man, who has a soft voice and brown eyes. I see the Thames, and the smiling plains of Blackheath. I listen and pray at my chamber-door as my father talks to you in our little cabinet of studies. I look from my window and see you depart" (1:29). After this letter showing how long-lasting that early attachment proved to be, it is not so easy to dismiss Thomas Newcome's love affair with a daughter of the old French aristocracy. Thackeray's narrative strategy, drawing on successful techniques of his earlier novels, continually requires the reader to alter and revise his vision of major fictional events, to see the same "old story" in new lights.

In addition to such deliberate variations in point of view, the reader's fundamental response to *The Newcomes* is also governed by the nature of the familiar events that make up Thackeray's "old story."[8] The most basic, recurring, and significant actions of this satire on Victorian social life are its meetings and partings: the opening assembly in the "Cave of Harmony," visits to Park Lane and Mrs. Honeyman's, gatherings at Mrs. Ridley's, the Colonel's arrivals from and departures to India, the "Congress at Baden," meetings at the Hotel de Florac, Clive and J.J.'s flight from Paris, encounters in Rome, trips to Rosebury and Newcome and London, the Colonel's many dinners around the silver coconut tree, the final coming together and parting at Grey Friars.[9] Similarly, in his ongoing experience of the novel, the reader is continually involved in meetings—coming closer to particular people of this fictional world—and partings—separations from the characters and author of Fable-land. In all such flurries of coming and going, a desire to escape, to reach a resting point outside the flux, comes to animate many characters, perhaps Ethel Newcome most of all: "Many a

111

splendid assembly, and many a brilliant next year, will the ardent and hopeful young creature enjoy; but in the midst of her splendor and triumphs, buzzing flatterers, conquered rivals, prostrate admirers, no doubt she will think sometimes of that quiet season before the world began for her, and that dear old friend [the Colonel] on whose arm she leaned while she was yet a young girl" (1:205). As the reader too hurries from assembly to assembly in his temporal reading experience, he also seeks resting places, moments in which he glimpses the pattern of events in this world. Such moments are provided for in the text in one sense simply by the enforced pauses of serial reading, a facet of *The Newcomes* to which I will return. But there are also moments in the fiction when the present action recalls similar previous ones, creating momentary pauses in the rush of ordinary experience. Much of Thackeray's narrative is deliberately designed to minimize particularities of time and space in order to encourage just such moments of generalized experience, moments that highlight Thackeray's version of the "human story."[10]

Specific places that figure again and again in the novel, for instance, become symbolically important, standing frequently more for frames of mind than physical locations, traditional stages in man's common pilgrimage. Grey Friars, that "ancient foundation of the time of James I., still subsisting in the heart of London city" (2:374). is, for example, a fixed point of reference for many of the novel's characters. The Colonel, Clive, Pendennis, and others went to school there, and it provides the setting of the novel's famous concluding scene, for "at that ancient institution is a college for old men as well as for boys" (1:134). As an unchanging point of reference in a changing world, a reminder of England's cultural heritage and the innocence of youth, Grey Friars reinforces the novel's principal theme of the changeless human story. Juliet McMaster has discussed how the different generations of the novel share many such key experiences: "The narrative structure itself re-echoes this theme: for Pen as narrator watches Clive going through the same agonies and perplexities, with a few years' time lag, that he had himself suffered in the progress from boyhood at Grey Friars to manhood in London, with all the challenges and pains of entering society and a profession, and falling in love."[11] When he returns for the first time from his years in India, the Colonel's presence links his own youth with his son's: "He dismissed his cab at Ludgate Hill, and walked thence by the dismal precincts of Newgate, and across the muddy pavement of Smithfield, on his way back to the old school where his son was, a way which he had trodden many a time in his own early days. . . . There was Thomas Newcome arrived in the middle of life, standing between the shouting boys and the tottering seniors, and in a situation to moralize upon both . . ." (1:70–71). The Colonel stands not so much at a point in space as at a point in time.

The capacity of places like Grey Friars to underscore the universality of human experience inspires many of the novel's moments of broadening perspective. When Pendennis, for example, returns to Grey Friars one Founder's Day because "the pupils educated there love to revisit it" (2:374), his vision of the human story deepens:

> We oldsters, be we ever so old, become boys again as we look at that familiar old tomb [the Founder's], and think how the seats are altered since we were here, and how the doctor—not the present doctor, the doctor of *our* time—used to sit yonder, and his awful eye used to frighten us shuddering boys, on whom it lighted. . . . A plenty of candles lights up this chapel, and this scene of age and youth, and early memories, and pompous death. How solemn the well-remembered prayers are, here uttered again in the place where in childhood we used to hear them! How beautiful and decorous the rite; how noble the ancient words of the supplications which the priest utters, and to which generations of fresh children and troops of bygone seniors have cried Amen! under those arches! (2:375)

The frequently satirical or cynical Pendennis suddenly sees his own life here in the larger context of English history, and the inspired panegyric on tradition makes his broadened perspective available to his readers as well. Repeated actions, then, in similar or identical places through a number of generations make up the substance of

The Newcomes; each time an event recurs, Thackeray's careful manipulation of point of view manages both to emphasize its particularity and to reveal its universality.[12]

Not only are there certain places like Grey Friars that come to mean the same thing for succeeding generations, there are also particular people whose presences assume universal importance in Thackeray's "old story" and remind the reader of broader contexts surrounding important events. Sarah Mason, the nurse of young Thomas Newcome (later the Colonel) and his mother's cousin, comes to represent the true past of the Newcome family. Her presence in the text recalls the common origin of the Newcome house in contrast to the exalted image assumed by most of this *nouveau riche* family (like the greatness Isabella had asserted for the Esmond family position). Although some Newcomes pretend to a genealogy beginning with a surgeon-barber to King Edward the Confessor, the true founder of the family whose history becomes Pendennis's narrative is Thomas Newcome, a weaver from the village of Newcome who came to London to seek his fortune in the time of George III. Prospering in his own business, he returned home for "a pretty girl whom he had left there, and whom he had promised to marry" (1:15). This act of loyalty to one he loved is responsible in part for the Newcome family fortune: "The whole country side was pleased to think of the prosperous London tradesman returning to keep his promise to the penniless girl whom he had loved in the days of his own poverty; the great country clothiers, who knew his prudence and honesty, gave him much of their business when he went back to London" (1:15). Although his second wife, Sophia Alethea Hobson (heiress to Hobson Brothers, cloth-factors) and her descendants consistently deny any family connection to Sarah, three generations of Newcomes admit their true family history, and thereby endorse such Old World qualities as love and loyalty responsible for their original success: Sarah eventually settles in a cottage in the north "with a liberal pension which Mr. Newcome gave her, and which his son [the Colonel] and his son's son [Clive] after him, through all their difficulties and distresses, always found means to pay" (1:21).

It is one of the early signs of Ethel Newcome's essential goodness that, unlike the rest of her branch of the family, she visits Sarah
Mason at Newcome. It is also symbolically appropriate that the
place where the Colonel snubs his favorite niece much later in the
novel is Sarah's cottage (2:298): the Colonel had taken Ethel's
earlier rejection of marriage to Clive as a sign of her unworthiness;
that both he and Ethel are visiting Sarah is a sign he should recognize that they now share kindred values. The Colonel's gradual fall
from the integrity he represents at the beginning of the novel is also
underscored by his evolving relationship to Sarah. Late in the history he allows Frederick Bayham to use his aunt as a political tool in
the revengeful campaign to take the Newcome seat in Parliament
from Barnes: on the polling day, a carriage appears at the booths
"containing Frederick Bayham, Esq., profusely decorated with the
Colonel's colours, and . . . old Mrs. Mason, who was pleased with
the drive and the sunshine, though she scarcely understood the
meaning . . ." (2:324). When, at her death, Sarah's annual pension
threatens to go to the Campaigner, Clive's terrible mother-in-law,
the reader sees the extent of the world's corruption of the values the
Colonel inherited from the past.

Not only does Sarah Mason's presence in the text establish a
fixed point of reference for the Newcome family, but her perspective on events reinforces in another way the novel's insistence on a
changeless human story. In her old age, she tends increasingly to
mix up generations, confusing Clive and the Colonel. Early in the
novel, for example, the Colonel takes Clive to visit his aunt:

> She embraced Clive still more eagerly and frequently than she kissed
> his father. She did not know her Colonel with them whiskers. Clive
> was the very picture of the dear boy as he had left her almost two-
> score years ago. And as fondly as she hung on the boy, her memory
> had ever clung round that early time when they were together. . . .
> Again and again she would think he was actually her own boy, forget-
> ting, in that sweet and pious hallucination, that the bronzed face, and
> thinned hair, and melancholy eyes of the veteran before her, were
> those of her nursling of old days." (1:162)

115

Sarah's senile wanderings do more than represent the weakening of traditional values in contemporary Victorian society, however. After all, the Colonel himself, the novel's most successful and remembered character, arrives at a state of mind remarkably like Sarah's by the end of the fiction: after the collapse of his fortune, the "torture had been too much for that kind old heart: there were times when Thomas Newcome passed beyond it. What still maddened Clive, excited his father no more; the pain yonder woman [Mrs. Mackenzie] inflicted, only felled and stupefied him" (2:403). As a pensioner at Grey Friars, the Colonel escapes his present difficulties by drifting, like Sarah, into confused memories of earlier times. Although this is clearly a breakdown in ordinary relationships to reality, some transcendence of time and space has also been a goal toward which the entire narrative has been reaching—an all-encompassing vision of times past, present, and future, the single vision of the "human story."

Although Sarah and the Colonel pay too high a price for this freedom from the confusing pace of modern life, theirs is only an extreme instance of a central desire in the novel: many of the major characters yearn for that moment in the past when the dreams of youth, particularly love, have not been disappointed by the real world.[13] Much of the narrative's fundamental drive, therefore, is toward this central moment in the "human story," at which the dream is either realized or passed by forever. Clive at one point identifies the clue to the entire family's fate: he calls the failure to seize that dream by marrying for love "fatal; it runs in the family, father" (2:313). As Clive and Ethel, Thomas and Léonore discover, the denial of love for material prosperity or social success marks a watershed in private history: everything seems to exist either before—when the heart lived in hope—or after—when the heart lives in memory. The perspective most insistently offered the reader by the novel's many narrators becomes, then, a "reminiscential vision," as Myron Taube has termed it.[14] Madame de Florac, for instance, spends her old age fixed on a moment decades earlier, as she writes to Thomas Newcome: "Did it not seem once as if [our] two hands never could unlock, so closely were they enlaced together? Ah, mine

116

are old and feeble now; forty years have passed since the time when you used to say they were young and fair. How well I remember me of every one of those days . . ." (2:165). And the Colonel's memory too continually reaches back to that time before love was denied: he writes his son years later, "in wandering forty years through the world since, I have seen no woman in my eyes so good or so beautiful" (2:10).

Because Thackeray's vision of human affairs insists that the younger Newcome generation is acting out the same "old story" already experienced by the senior, Clive and Ethel can present in the dramatic present this central moment in the Colonel and Madame de Florac's past. Chapter 47, "Two or Three Acts of a Little Comedy," perhaps the best in the novel, embodies the central moment of Thackeray's "old story," the midpoint of the major characters' lives toward which the reader's attention is directed again and again in the novel.[15] The scene is appropriately Keatsian, where, as on the Grecian urn, the moment of bliss is not quite fully realized but neither is it yet passed: "There is Cupid, who has been at the point of kissing Psyche this half-century at least, though the delicious event has never come off through all those blazing summers and dreary winters . . ." (2:93). In between the several dialogues of Clive and Ethel, Madame de Florac appears, reminding Ethel and the reader of the doubling of generations: "when I see a young girl who may be made the victim—the subject of a marriage of convenience, as I was—my heart pities her. And if I love her, as I love you, I tell her my thoughts. Better poverty, Ethel—better a cell in a convent, than a union without love" (2:102). In the crucial encounters that the chapter presents, then, Clive plays not only himself but his father courting the young Léonore de Blois, as Ethel takes on the role of Thomas Newcome's first love as well as Clive's. The disappearance of the novel's usual narrator reinforces the universal nature of the drama, leaving for the reader the task of articulating the timeworn context of these events. Clive and Ethel embody the eternal young couple in love, acting out the central conflict of the Newcome family history, the pull of natural affection against the temptations of a materialistic society. Clive offers to carry Ethel "to

117

the end of the world" (2: 106), but Ethel refuses to renounce her pledge to marry according to her family's wishes and secure a fortune: "I won't say a word about the—the regard which you express for me. I think you have it. Indeed, I do. But it were best not said, Clive; best for me, perhaps, not to own that I know it. In your speeches, my poor boy—and you will please not to make any more, or I never can see you or speak to you again, never—you forgot one part of a girl's duty: obedience to her parents" (2:110). From this exchange we can predict much of their future lives. Back toward this moment will Ethel and Clive look for the rest of the novel, as indeed they have looked forward to it in preceding sections.

Many other characters in *The Newcomes* engage in attempts to recapture the past, frequently providing for the reader similar sudden glimpses of the novel's whole design. One of the most memorable moments that encapsulate the "human story" is the Colonel's first meeting with Ethel, whose "youth, and modesty, and beauty" (1:166) reveal that the Colonel has never forgotten his first love. As his mind plays back and forth between past and present, stimulating further reflections by the narrator, the reader glimpses the full scope of the Colonel's (and Ethel's) story:

> There was no point of resemblance, and yet a something in the girl's look, voice, and movements, which caused his heart to thrill, and an image out of the past to rise up and salute him. The eyes which had brightened his youth (and which he saw in his dreams and thoughts for faithful years afterwards, as though they looked at him out of heaven) seemed to shine upon him after five-and-thirty years. . . . It is an old saying, that we forget nothing; as people in fever begin suddenly to talk the language of their infancy, we are striken by memory sometimes, and old affections rush back on us as vivid as in the time when they were our daily talk, when their presence gladdened our eyes, when their accents thrilled in our ears, when with passionate tears and grief we flung ourselves upon their hopeless corpses. Parting is death, at least as far as life is concerned. A passion comes to an end; it is carried off in a coffin, or weeping in a post-chaise; it drops out of life one way or other, and the earth-clods close over it, and we see it no more. But it has been part of our souls, and it is eternal. Does a

118

mother not love her dead infant? a man his lost mistress? with the fond wife nestling at his side,—yes, with twenty children smiling round her knee. No doubt as the old soldier held the girl's hand in his, the little talisman led him back to Hades, and he saw Léonore. (1:166)

As though looking at him "out of heaven," Léonore has dominated the Colonel's innermost emotional life, almost as a divine force. Thackeray's "old saying," like his "old story" itself, insists that "we forget nothing," particularly not such key moments that define the shape of a long life. The elevation of personal relationships here to a kind of spiritual truth ("it has been part of our souls, and it is eternal") is appropriate to this secular novel; it also suggests the intensity of the Colonel's love for Léonore, and the terrible finality of his parting from her. Returned now to that "Hades" free of time and space, the remembered past where such moments remain eternal, the Colonel could not deny the truth his son later discovers also—"once means always in these things, father, doesn't it? Once means to-day, and yesterday, and for ever and ever" (2:313).

The paradoxical statement at the heart of this passage—"Parting is death, at least as far as life is concerned"—sums up the novel's worldly theology: to separate from one you love is to accept a kind of death. Léonore reflects on the years of separation from her days with Thomas Newcome: "there is a death between me and them, and it is as across a grave I review them" (2:165). Watching the Colonel return to India, Pendennis reflects on the traditional hope that the pain of the many partings that dominate his text will one day be answered: "Ah, pangs of hearts torn asunder, passionate regrets, cruel cruel partings! Shall you not end one day, ere many years; when the tears shall be wiped from all eyes, and there shall be neither sorrow nor pain" (1:279). And reflecting on Léonore's "nearly fifty years dying," Pen anticipates the climactic final scene of the novel: "If love lives through all life; and survives through all sorrow; and remains steadfast with us through all changes; and in all darkness of spirit burns brightly; and, if we die, deplores us for ever, and loves still equally; and exists with the very last gasp and

119

throb of the faithful bosom—whence it passes with the pure soul, beyond death; surely it shall be immortal! Though we who remain are separated from it, is it not ours in heaven? If we love still those we lose, can we altogether lose those we love?" (2:81). But such otherworldly solutions remain beyond the pale of this social novel, merely questions, however passionately asked, in Pendennis's text. Only in memory can the past be relived, can the inevitable partings of life be overcome in the mind's simultaneous grasp of past and present.

Part of the Colonel's sadness when he is "back in common life" (1:166) after his memorable meeting with Ethel is the realization that this new generation is about to undergo the same suffering he and Madame de Florac have already endured, that the "old story" is about to be reenacted. When he later tells his son of his love for Léonore and its disappointment, he provides us with another compressed image of the "human story" as he has come to know it. "Your cousin Ethel reminded me of her: as handsome, but not so *lovely*. Yes, it was that pale lady you saw at Paris, with eyes full of care, and hair streaked with grey. So it will be the turn of you young folks, come eight more *lustres,* and your heads will be bald like mine, or gray like Madame de Florac's, and bending over the ground where we are lying in quiet" (2:10). This telescopic vision of the old story of love accurately predicts the novel's future. At one of Barnes's political speeches late in the novel, Clive encounters a vision of the past much like his father's: "the past and its dear histories, and youth and its hopes and passions, and tones and looks for ever echoing in the heart, and present in the memory—these, no doubt, poor Clive saw and heard as he looked across the great gulf of time, and parting and grief, and beheld the woman he had loved for many years. There [Ethel] sits; the same, but changed; as gone from him as if she were dead; departed indeed into another sphere, and entered into a kind of death" (2:300). In this essential metaphor of the novel, Ethel and Clive, like Thomas and Léonore, have parted at the moment of life where love was to have been gained and are now forever separated by a deathlike chasm. That realm of memory where they can be together again remains the only hope of the novel itself, the final perspective offered the reader from which human events can be shaped into a desirable pattern.

Every time the power of memory asserts itself in *The Newcomes*, however, there comes a recognition of its limitations; for despite the remarkable force of memory in Thackeray, he knows that in one sense it remains a futile activity, an attempt to escape the hard world of the present. All the letters, papers, and other material Pen uses in his history of the Newcome family become symbols of the inspiring but unattainable past:

> In the faded ink, on the yellow paper that may have crossed and recrossed oceans, that has lain locked in chests for years, and buried under piles of family archives, while your friends have been dying and your head has grown white—who has not disinterred mementoes like these—from which the past smiles at you so sadly, shimmering out of Hades an instant but to sink back again into the cold shades, perhaps with a faint faint sound as of a remembered tone—a ghostly echo of a once familiar laughter?" (1:295)

Dominated by images of death, this passage illustrates the melancholy sadness that in the end underscores the entire family history. The backward look so frequently offered us by the narrative proves again and again to be illusory; all the characters must return to the "common life" of the present or—like Sarah Mason and the Colonel—escape into unreality.

The use of "Hades" as a symbol of this irretrievable past appears not only here and in the central image of the Colonel's first meeting with Ethel, but also in the novel's conclusion, the famous last scene at Grey Friars Hospital. As a desirable but ultimately inaccessible realm, this "Hades" of memory seems to mark the perspective on human events most encouraged by the novel's shifting and expanding points of view, but in the end we are as conscious of our separation from it as our participation in it. This perspective is, of course, the product of the readers' consistency-building, as is the understanding of family and national history in *Henry Esmond,* and can be best achieved only after the novel is over; but the recurring

121

images of memory in the text are formal manifestations of this important theme.

Thomas Newcome's final parting in this life is an appropriate conclusion to a long novel full of memorable partings, even though it frequently appears sentimental to modern readers. But Gordon Ray is still right that the novel's length and its serial format encourage an experience not always realized by twentieth-century readers:

> Certainly of all Thackeray's novels it is the one which benefited most from the circumstances of serial issue. As it appeared in twenty-four monthly parts, it seemed to many readers the "masterpiece of all novel writing." Such an audience was not disturbed by its slow beginning, by the "seated mass of information" which requires a sixth of the novel before the narrative proper begins. This prolonged exposition is necessary preparation for the rest, in which, as Thackeray promised, "there's plenty of action & passion too"; but only slow, concentrated attention, such as serial readers were prepared to give, could ensure its proper assimilation.[16]

It is not only the serial reader's attention to detail that helps him get to "know the Newcomes as well as any family in fiction" (Ray, *Age of Wisdom*, p. 237); each monthly part also involves a widening of perspectives on significant repeated actions, Thackeray's "old story" carefully presented in new lights.

The reader's "assimilation" of the novel is further aided by the rhythm of reading in monthly installments, which involves repeated, fresh encounters with the fiction's characters. Beginning each number after a month's absence is for the reader getting to know the characters all over again—recalling from past reading experiences important characteristics, actions, and ideas—in much the same way the people of the fiction make their acquaintances with each other through repeated meetings. The perspective of memory—in which past and present are held simultaneously in view—becomes for the serial reader especially, as for the characters, a necessary point of view. With intimacy reestablished in any number, readers soon find they must face another parting, the end of the monthly installment. And in a novel constructed of meetings and partings like *The Newcomes,* the reader thus becomes caught up in the same activity as the novel's characters. The ends of each short fiction become more and more like little deaths for readers and author, as the characters must remain in a remembered world and the audience must turn to its own world for thirty days of a different life.

The theme of separation—of characters from each other, of characters from reader, of reader from author—emphasized by both content and form in *The Newcomes,* is, of course, a familiar one in the Victorian period. As Walter Houghton observes, Victorians were "acutely conscious of separation. They felt isolated by dividing barriers; lonely for a lost companionship, human and divine; nostalgic for an earlier world of country peace and unifying belief."[17] The separation of reader from author and fictional world which ends each monthly number in the serial novel is a part of the entire age's sense of lost community relationships. The sentimental desire to return to the world of the fiction and to unify all its characters is a fundamental impulse for the nineteenth-century parts reader. Jerome Beaty has suggested such an "analogy between parts publication and the Victorian worldpicture";[18] I find the Victorians' appreciation of sentimental deaths and partings clearly related to the long-term but regularly interrupted commitment to their fictional worlds required by the temporal form of serial publication. It is not surprising, then, that *The Newcomes*'s final scene of separation was particularly wrenching for the original audience, as well as for the author of the fiction.[19] They had suffered twenty-two partings already, and knew this one to be more final than any, reminding them once more of the Victorian period's sense (in Houghton's terms) of "cosmic isolation and the terror of absolute solitude."[20]

With the characters doubling in essential roles and the setting that universal home Grey Friars, the final scene gathers together all the key elements of Thackeray's "old story" in a final tableau. Become "a youth again" (2:419), the Colonel confuses Ethel with Léonore, Boy with Clive: "Now, as in those early days, his heart was pure; no anger remained in it; no guile tainted it; only peace and good-will dwelt in it" (2:419). Escaping the confines of time and space, the Colonel takes himself back to that key moment in his life, when he and Léonore were the eternal young couple in love. "Toujours, toujours!" (2:420), he cries, holding Ethel's hand but believing it to be Léonore's, back at that dividing line in life where "Forever wilt thou love, and she be fair!" Although at the very end his "hands outside the bed feebly beat time" (2:421), and he claims to be present ("Adsum") at this time and place, the Colonel finally transcends the processes of time to become part of Thackeray's unrecoverable past: he "stood in the presence of The Master" (2:421), in the "Hades" of the novel where dreams are recovered.

The novel does not end here, of course, for the readers must be "taking leave" of this company, as Thomas Newcome, Pendennis, and all the others have just parted from us, convicting them to life in memory. Recalling the moment when he first realized the histories of "Pendennis and Laura and Ethel and Clive" (2:421), Thackeray himself speaks in the epilogue, placing his creatures in the same realm as his fiction's unattainable past: "They were alive, and I heard their voices; but five minutes since was touched by their grief. And have we parted with them here on a sudden, and without so much as a shake of the hand? Is yonder line (———) which I drew with my own pen, a barrier between me and Hades as it were, across which I can see those figures retreating and only dimly glimmering?" (2:421). Here the realms of fiction (Fable-land) and memory are linked by the name "Hades." Only in such worlds can human aspirations always be answered, can the "old story" be altered at the end to please us all: "the poet of Fable-land rewards and punishes absolutely. He splendidly deals out bags of sovereigns, which won't buy anything; belabours wicked backs with awful blows, which do not hurt; endows heroines with preternatural beauty, and creates heroes, who, if ugly sometimes, yet possess a thousand good qualities, and usually end by being immensely rich; makes the hero and heroine happy at last, and happy ever after" (2:423). From this "happy, harmless, Fable-land"—and from each other—Thackeray and his readers must now take farewell, and the final parting is at the same time trivial and tragic: trivial because no real pain is involved in this loss of an imaginary world, but tragic because we go through the motions of parting, a real event that, in Thackeray's and his age's view, is an inescapable fact of life outside of fiction. Thackeray's "lingering hold" on his reader's hand at the end of *The Newcomes*, then, involves not only the close relationship of serial novelist and reader we have long known existed in Victorian literature. The author is also reluctant to let go because it means his own departure; he must now leave the realm of fiction where dreams can be answered in ways the real world, to which he is returning, cannot. He must abandon the satisfactory perspective on human events his narrative has pursued, and at times achieved.

Thackeray shaped each of his twenty-three meetings with his reader artfully, of course, keeping each strand of plot and group of characters active in every number.[21] But that literary expertise alone does not account for this novel's popularity in its time, nor its dimmed reputation in ours. Recalling, however, one essential difference between the original readers' experience and our own— their two-year, regularly interrupted involvement with the text— gives us some helpful clues in understanding this novel, and other mid-Victorian classics. Victorian readers encountered in a thirty-two-page part of Thackeray's *The Newcomes* not only new developments of plot but an expanding frame of reference in which to view those events. In each encounter with the characters, the readers discover new particularities about them and their situation, while gradually coming to see the universal "human story" underlying them. And at the heart of all monthly reading lies, I believe, the repeated awareness of one central fact of Thackeray's vision, the inevitable separation from the dreams and loves of youth that time forces on us—Thomas Newcome's departure for India as Léonore de Blois marries the Comte de Florac, Clive's turning to Rosey Mackenzie as Ethel refuses to break with Lady Kew. Although memory persistently tries to rewrite the past, the narrative cannot escape the shape of what has already been completed. The conclusions of the monthly numbers and the final scene itself of this "great loose baggy monster" become powerful reminders of a primary fact of Thackeray's "old story" and the Victorian world-view—the end.

As final as this emphasis seems to be, however, reading Thackeray is not over at the end of any part or with the whole of *The Newcomes*. The rhythm of Victorian life, which the author has captured in his fiction, insists that there be more reading Thackeray. Essential to the ideology of Victorian literature, that is, is a belief in the future that refuses to find any ending absolute. This open-endedness in the nineteenth-century novel is visible even in Thackeray's last, unfinished work, *Denis Duval*.

6
Literary Pieces and Whole Audiences

At the time of his death in December 1863 Thackeray was at work on a novel intended to appear in eight magazine installments. As much of *Denis Duval* as he had written appeared posthumously in four issues of *Cornhill* magazine from March until June 1864. Similarly, six of the projected twelve monthly numbers of Dickens's *The Mystery of Edwin Drood* appeared from April to September 1870. The third number was out at the time of Dickens's sudden death from a stroke, though two more numbers—and most of the sixth— had already been written. And forty-eight of the planned sixty chapters in Trollope's *The Landleaguers* had been completed at his death on 6 December 1882; they appeared in *Life: A Weekly Journal of Society, Literature, the Fine Arts and Finance* from 16 November 1882 until 4 October 1883. These unfinished novels have literary value of a kind often overlooked by modern criticism. How Victorians read Thackeray's *Denis Duval* was determined by certain established assumptions about literature and the age not always acknowledged in contemporary literary scholarship. These nineteenth-century assumptions can best be perceived by viewing this one unfinished work within the larger class of all three novels.

To begin with, these unfinished fictions were widely read and discussed by reviewers (and readers) of the major literary periodicals of the day, despite the fact that they were incomplete. Dickens, for instance, recommended the text of *Denis Duval* to the

Victorian audience, finding "an approach to completeness in the fragment."[1] Trollope found the reading of *Denis Duval* similarly worthwhile: ". . . his forthcoming novel was anxiously looked for by many. . . . I think that those concerned in the matter will be adjudged to be right in giving to the public so much of this work as he has left behind him."[2] Some journals, following Trollope's reasoning, included *Denis Duval* as a major work in their summations of Thackeray's career. For instance, the *Home and Foreign Review* (April 1864) observes:

> The fragment published displays extraordinary care; and characters, like those of Agnes' parents, which must be quite subsidiary to the main business of the plot, are finished miniatures. In Clarisse's catastrophe we see a version of a tragical incident which occurred a few years ago in the English literary world at Paris, interpreted according to the medico-psychological doctrines of Mr. Lewis. Denis himself was to be a great muscular sailor, approaching still nearer to Mr. Kingsley's ideal than Philip; and Agnes was to be his guardian angel, just as Laura was to Pendennis. . . . (P. 493)

And the *Spectator* (5 March 1864) says that ". . . the fragment leaves on us an indefinable impression as if Mr. Thackeray had succeeded in bringing to the surface that deep tenderness which all who knew him believe to have underlain his outwardly sarcastic habit. There is a gentle mellowness in his writing hardly so conspicuous before, or rather conspicuous only in passages, instead of flavouring, as in this instance, entire chapters" (p. 274).

Less specifically literary voices also directed their readers to Thackeray's last work at the time of its first publication. The *Illustrated Times* (5 March 1864) commended Thackeray's unfinished work to its audience: "'Denis Duval' leads off [*Cornhill*] and keeps so far above the level of merely occasional criticism that the kind reader will excuse any words of 'praise'" (p. 218). The *Press* (5 March 1864) echoed the general enthusiasm: "The first four chapters [of *Denis Duval*] are contained in this number of the *The Cornhill*, and we venture to say that they have been read with intense interest by every one. . . . These four chapters form in themselves almost a complete picture . . ." (p. 236).

Henry James, writing a generation later in *Scribner's Magazine* in January 1901 recalls this remarkable enthusiasm for the original publication of *Duval:*

> I remember, after all, perfectly, the poetry of its original appearance— there was a thrill, in those days, even after "Lovel the Widower" and "Philip," at any new Thackeray—in the cherished "Cornhill" of the early time, with a drawing of Frederick Walker to its every number and a possibility of its being like "Esmond" in its embroidered breast. If, moreover, it after a few months broke short off, that really gave it something as well as took something away. It might have been as true of works of art as of men and women, that if the gods loved them they died young. "Denis Duval" was at any rate beautiful, and was beautiful again on reperusal at a later time.[3]

What such an unfinished novel "gave," rather than what it "took away," for its Victorian audience is my subject here.

Reaction to Trollope's unfinished novel also points to a Victorian interest in fragments, although, as Robert Tracey points out, "reviewers were not very enthusiastic about *The Landleaguers.* . . ."[4] Trollope's reputation had declined somewhat late in his career, of course, and the admission in his *Autobiography* that he wrote mechanically, by the clock, further undermined his standing among critics, as this comment by the *Academy* shows: "Such books [as *The Landleaguers*] we could only read—as we now know for certain they were written—as conscientious task work at so much a page and so many pages a day."[5] Still, the words of any major writer were bound to receive some attention, as the *Spectator* argued at the time: Trollope "was certainly eminent enough to make the public anxious to have all that he wrote, and especially the very last work that came from his pen."[6] And several reviews find the novel deserving of praise even though it is unfinished. The *Saturday Review* says, "The *truncum corpus* of the book is, despite this drawback [of incompleteness], far from unpleasant to read as a novel. . . ."[7] Similarly, the editors of

129

the *Athenaeum* find it "more interesting than the generality of his books" and assume that their subscribers at least will take the time to read the work: "Leaving these matters for the reader to discover, we may say that the plot centres in the fortune of the Jones family and their neighbours in county Galway."[8]

Although the consideration given to Trollope's and Thackeray's unfinished works by literary periodicals was widespread, the attention accorded Dickens's *Drood* was even greater, particularly in the popular press.[9] The Victorian readers' enthusiasm is first for new installments in a novel they think will be completed, as Dickens's death comes unexpectedly after the publication of the third number.[10] Still, the involvement with Dickens's work remains consistent throughout the full run of *Drood*'s six monthly installments.[11] While it is certainly true that his great reputation and popularity made Dickens's fragments more appealing than those of any other author, the artistic principles that underlie these periodicals' approach to *Drood* apply to Victorian fiction in general: being in the midst of a long novel is as rewarding as having arrived at its conclusion. Reading *Denis Duval*, even in 1864, then, did not mean closing out Thackeray's career in the way we tend to think of it today because his work ends, in a sense, in the middle.

The critical theory of Wolfgang Iser again helps us to understand reading Thackeray, identifying the aspect of plot that is especially effective in unfinished novels like Thackeray's *Denis Duval*. Iser's aim in part is to "halt the time-flow of reading" and to analyze "one paradigmatic reading moment."[12] He discusses at length the way in which a reader is "building images" at every moment of his reading. Further, Iser points out that the "reader's position in the text is at the point of intersection between retention and protension" (p. 111), between looking back at things that have happened in the text that has been read, and looking forward to things that may happen in the text still to be read. "Each individual sentence correlate prefigures a particular horizon," continues Iser; "but this is immediately transformed into the background for the next correlate and must therefore necessarily be modified." That is, what we imagine might happen next at any single moment in a novel changes continuously as we

130

move forward in reading, as does our understanding of what has happened. Iser then stresses how the reader's movement in a text also involves ambiguity: "Since each sentence correlate aims at things to come, the prefigured horizon will offer a view which—however concrete it may be—must contain indeterminacies. . . . In most literary texts . . . the sequence of sentences is so structured that the correlates serve to modify and even frustrate the expectations they have aroused" (p. 111). In other words, according to Iser, more expectations are aroused at any moment of a literary text than can ever be resolved.

The aspect of plot identified by Iser—"image building" or the creation of possibilities in the reader's mind at each moment in the plot—is, I think, a central feature of Thackeray's *Denis Duval* and other unfinished novels of the last century, as well as of Victorian novels in general. A. E. Dyson arrives at a similar point as a digression in his important analysis of *Drood:*

> We must accept, however reluctantly, that certain of [Dickens's] intentions remain inaccessible, and that areas of doubt about the projected denouement will always remain. There is in this (to digress a little) an accidental insight about "inevitability," in so far as we often feel retrospective "inevitability" about a major work of art in its finished state. If *Edwin Drood* had been completed, it would surely have struck us like this, since what we have of it demonstrates such a rare unity of mood and growth. Yet when it breaks off, conflicting possibilities remain very evidently open, as if to confirm the actual laws of organic growth.[13]

Recovering this feature of plot—its quality of opening out in many directions of possibility—and exploring what that provides for the reader raises our estimate of the Victorian authors' achievement in fiction. Not only is image building an important element in the structure of *Denis Duval* and other unfinished Victorian novels, but it is also a central theme. I wish to consider first this thematic concern, and then return to some questions about the form of Victorian fiction.

131

At one point in Thackeray's last novel the hero and narrator, Denis Duval, comments on how as a child he looked up to the light in the window of the girl he loved and how that image has remained a guiding force in his life:

> I saw my dearest little maiden's light glimmering in her chamber, and the stars shining overhead, and felt—who could feel more bold and happy than I.
>
> That walk schoolwards by West Street certainly was a *détour*. I might have gone a straighter road, but then I should not have seen *a certain window:* a little twinkling window in a gable of the Priory House, where the light used to be popped out at nine o'clock. T'other day, when we took over the King of France to Calais (his Royal Highness the Duke of Clarence being in command), I must needs hire a post-chaise from Dover, to look at that old window in the Priory House at Winchelsea. I went through the old tears, despairs, tragedies. I sighed as sentimentally, after forty years, as though the *infandi dolores* were fresh upon me, as though I were the schoolboy trudging back to his task, and taking a last look at his dearest joy. I used as a boy to try and pass that window at nine, and I know a prayer was said for the inhabitant of yonder chamber. She knew my holidays, and my hours of going to school and returning hence. If my little maid hung certain signals in that window (such as a flower, for example, to indicate all was well, a cross-curtain, and so forth), I hope she practised no very unjustifiable stratagems. (P. 517)[14]

Like Iser's hypothetical reader, Thackeray's young protagonist was "building images" of the future he might possess while he looked up at Agnes's window, as was, of course, Agnes when she displayed a flower there. Through the window of his own narrative, the older Denis Duval at the end of his life recalls that same window, savoring the hope for the future his younger self enjoyed. Even more, the older Denis literally revisits the spot at which he contemplated that window and his future in order to sustain the feeling that he is at an early, promising point in his life's journey.

In other places of the novel, this looking to a window similarly expresses a desire to understand the past and to anticipate the future. On his memorable journey to London, for instance, the young

Denis Duval looks out the chaise window and into other windows, spotting individuals who have endorsed his prospects: "I see dear Mrs. Barnard's great cap nodding at us out of the parlour window as we drive away from the Rectory door to stop a hundred yards farther on at the Priory" (p. 402). With the tense changed in his narrative from past to present, the older Duval reviewing his life again places Agnes near both the beginning and the end of his journey through life: "There at the parlour window stands my dear little Agnes, in a white frock, in a great cap with a blue riband and bow, and curls clustering over her face" (p. 402).

As such images of promise recur in Thackeray's text, his Victorian readers could connect the protagonist's ultimate stability— married to Agnes and with a grown son—to their own. When Denis learns that war with France has broken out, for instance, he sees a light which suggests for him an ominous future, but for the reader a peaceful one. At the end of the third installment Duval writes that he and his school friends "could see the French lights across the Channel. My life has lasted for fifty years since then, and scarcely ever since, but for very, very brief intervals, has that baleful war-light ceased to burn" (p. 535). From Denis's present (the 1820s), however, until Thackeray's present (1864), peace has reigned between England and the Continent, and Victorian readers would see their own future as a bright prospect. That images of lights and windows come to be associated with the audience's own future might also be evident in *Cornhill*'s editorial notes about the unwritten portions of Thackeray's narrative. Imagining Duval's reunion with Agnes after his military days, the editor wonders whether it might not be "in the old familiar haunts [such as] the plain from whence they could see the French lights across the Channel; the little twinkling window in a gable of the priory house, where the light used to be popped out at nine o'clock—that Denis and Agnes first met after their long separation?" (p. 664). Having the bright prospect of eventual stability and security seems a fundamental goal of Thackeray's characters in *Denis Duval*.

In Dickens's unfinished last work, similarly, images of the future recur frequently. For example, some six months after Edwin

Drood's disappearance (the central event of the novel), Mr. Grewgious stands late one night at a window in his apartment contemplating the London landscape. Mr. Grewgious figures in this instance even more pointedly than Denis Duval as a reader, standing at that point where past and future intersect: ". . . his gaze wandered," we read, "from the windows to the stars, as if he would have read in them something that was hidden from him. Many of us would if we could; but none of us so much as know our letters in the stars yet—or seem likely to do it, in this state of existence—and few languages can be read until their alphabets are mastered."[15] This passage seems pessimistic about man's ability to see the future, to know ends; but there is also here an expanse of space before Mr. Grewgious that represents opportunity or possibility, a key theme of the novel.

For Grewgious and for many of both novels' characters a future full of unknown possibilities is often more desirable than knowledge of how life's journey may end. John Jasper, for example, feels himself "daily drudging round" (p. 10) in circles at his job. His visits to London and an opium supplier underscore his desire to escape his fixed course in life. Jasper also resents the younger Neville Landless because his future is open: "The world is all before [Landless] where to choose. A life of stirring work and interest . . ." (p. 50), he says. Edwin Drood complains (before he disappears) to his uncle and guardian that his life too is "laid down to scale, and lined and dotted our for [me], like a surveyor's plan" (p. 9). His career in engineering and his engagement to young Rosa Bud had been prearranged by his father before his death, causing Drood's dissatisfaction with his fixed lot. And Rosa, whose parents are also dead and whose future too has been planned for her, regrets that it "*is* so absurd to be an engaged orphan" (p. 15). A central action of the novel is these two young characters' decision to break free of the futures planned for them by others.

Similarly, Thackeray's chief characters resent entrapment in a single, predicted course. Clarisse, Agnes's mother, hated her marriage to the Count de Saverne so much that she ran away when he was about to return from war and resume their life together. Desiring any alternative to that future, she sits full of fear in the home of Denis's mother (the childhood friend to whom she has fled) and looks into the distance as do so many characters in both novels. She would "go to the window . . . and look to the sea. For hours she sate at that window, with a curtain twisted round her, as if hiding from some one" (p. 282). Clarisse fears a return to her fixed course in life and the loss of such an open prospect.

Her husband, writing to Clarisse while away on military service before her flight, also envisioned a future of opportunity, but for the child his wife was expecting, not himself. Denis recalls: "I have read many letters of his which he sent from Corsica to his wife, and which she kept. They were full of strange minute orders, as to the rearing and education of this son that was to be born. . . . In these letters, I remember, the events of the campaign were dismissed in a very few words: the main part of the letters consisted of prayers, speculations, and prophecies regarding the child, and sermons couched in the language of the writer's stern creed" (p. 265). The count's horror at his wife and child's having become Catholic, and the anti-Catholic feelings Denis sees throughout his world, are connected to a fear of an unalterable course in life. M. de Saverne reads the register record of the event "with an awful grief in his face, and in a mood which I [M. Schnorr] heartily pitied": "on the 21st January, 1769, being the Feast of St. Agnes, the noble lady, Clarisse, Countess of Saverne, born de Viomesnil, aged twenty-two years, and Agnes, only daughter of the same Count of Saverne and Clarisse his wife, were baptized and received into the Church in the presence of two witnesses (clerics) whose names were signed" (p. 276).

Edwin Drood's disappearance, the central event in Dickens's novel, may be a result of his desire to choose another course in life, reinforcing the novel's theme of open futures. Edwin's fiancée, Rosa, keeps her hopes for an open future alive by fleeing from provincial Cloisterham to the city of London where she meets Tartar, who takes her for a boat ride on the Thames. On the river, her course seems agreeably open, as the "tide bore them on in the gayest and most sparkling manner" (p. 173). Our heroine, whose

135

name ("Rosa Bud") underscores this theme of potentiality, also finds a freer, if only imagined, future in "books of voyages and sea-adventure" (p. 177), which are read to her by her companion at her London residence. The wise Mr. Grewgious articulates this key theme of much Victorian fiction—the desire for an open future—when he says to Rosa, "one never knows in what direction a way out [of difficulty] may chance to open. It is a business principle of mine, in such a case, not to close up any direction, but to keep an eye on every direction that may present itself" (p. 161). Just as Denis Duval, Clarisse, the Count de Saverne, Grewgious, Jasper, Drood, and Rosa all desire such unlimited futures, so the Victorian citizen sought a life full of potential among the many expanding horizons of nineteenth-century life.

Roy Roussel comments on this aspect of the characters' situation in *Drood,* saying that Rosa and Jasper are "trapped in unfinished states."[16] Roussel finds this incompleteness central to the novel: "its unfinished state mirrors, in an uncanny way, its theme" (p. 402). He believes that the novel's "central question [is] the possibility of its characters completing or fulfilling their lives" (p. 384). Ina Rae Hark believes that marriage would have provided the completion for this novel as it did for so much of Victorian fiction:

> Whichever possibility Dickens might have chosen, the mystery of Rosa Bud's husband remains inextricable from the meaning of *The Mystery of Edwin Drood*. Either her marriage to Edwin (or Neville) after each had achieved a balance of inner and outer selves, or her final lack of a mate would be consistent with the development of Dickens's later fiction and with the thematic structure of the existing half of the novel[17]

Earle Davis agrees that the right marriage would be "a crowning expression of its themes and images."[18] Roussel, however, finds resolution unlikely for *Drood* because an "opposition between the narrative as a completed story and the narrative as an open-ended process was fundamental to Dickens's conception of *The Mystery of Edwin Drood*" (p. 385). Roussel claims that the novel is the author's

136

"search for alternative grounds for the text's completion" (p. 387), but "the act of writing opens out into a field of language which denies the centrality of the narrator who brings it into being" (p. 401); thus, completion is impossible. However, the open-ended-ness of this text, like that of Thackeray's, is its strength, not its weakness. These Victorian writers did not need to change their conception of the world or their language to create works of literary worth so much as we need to change our critical perspectives to discover the value that is already there in *Drood, Duval,* and *The Landleaguers.*[19]

One recurring feature of Thackeray's style in *Denis Duval* un-derscores the theme of the potential of any moment in time: the uncompleted sentence. And these unfinished sentences in the text represent the literary value of image building, as the reader is en-couraged to complete each construction. This stylistic device is sometimes used simply to heighten suspense, as when Denis and his mother are surprised by Clarisse's sudden appearance after she has fled her husband: "As the door opens, a great gust of wind sets our two candles flickering, and I see enter . . ." (p. 280). In this case, Thackeray's narrative gives us only a moment to complete the sen-tence before continuing: "A gentleman giving his arm to a lady" are the next words of the text. In other places, the completion is fairly obvious, though unstated. For instance, Clarisse writes to Denis's mother befores she leaves the count, "Have I come to be such monster as to wish my own husband . . . No. I wish I was" (p. 271).

These unfinished sentences are also consistent with thematic concerns of Thackeray's novel, as Denis, whose family is involved in illegal smuggling across the English Channel, is taught to leave some important matters in his world unstated. At one point, for instance, the young Denis is about "to explain the whole matter [of a fishing trip with his grandfather] artlessly to one of our neigh-bours who happened to step into supper, when grandpapa (who had made a grace of five minutes long before taking the dish-cover off) fetched me a slap across the face which sent me reeling" (p. 391). Denis had been describing how "we were hailed by my old

137

friend Bidois, who had come from Boulogne in his lugger—and then . . ." Thackeray's text stops here because Denis is forcefully prevented from going further; Denis is later told by de la Motte "Learn to hold thy little tongue, Denis, mon garçon!" (p. 392). Such moments add to Thackeray's questioning in the novel of honesty, honor, family loyalty, and patriotism. Denis's writing his own story is a final filling in the blanks for him, an open statement of the truth and his beliefs. He later notes: "There were matters connected with this story [of Denis's being unjustly accused of stealing] regarding which I *could* not speak. Should I do so, I must betray secrets which were not mine, and which implicated I knew not whom, and regarding which I must hold my piece. Now, they are secrets no more. That old society of smugglers is dissolved long ago: nay, I shall have to tell presently how I helped myself to break it up" (p. 526). This memoir, then, like Henry Esmond's, constitutes the protagonist's completion of all the parts of his life's story.

In his unfinished novel, Dickens also uses a particular stylistic device, the pause; and open-ended pauses in his text, like uncompleted sentences in *Duval,* represent the literary value of image building. An unusual number of characters in this last of Dickens's works pause in action, speech, or thought, just as Grewgious did in looking up at the stars. Miss Twinkleton, for instance, often comes to a "pause" (p. 97) in her addresses to the young ladies of the Nun's House. She must avoid allowing any indelicate word (like "bosom") to be heard instead of the proper term ("hearts"). While pauses in her little talks protect her from such indiscretion, they provide space for her audience to explore alternatives. The aggressive philanthropist, the Reverend Mr. Honeythunder, is also always "platformally pausing" (p. 131) as he assaults the unenlightened. Mrs. Billikin, who becomes Rosa's London landlady, also introduces "genteel pauses" (p. 171) in her speech and action to impress visitors.

These frequent pauses, which leave room for a listener's or reader's speculation, often occur against a backdrop of unfinished structures: Jasper's rooms contain an "unfinished picture of a blooming schoolgirl [Rosa]" (p. 6); the unusual character Durdles lives in a house "never finished" (p. 26); and the fatherly Mr. Crisparkle and Neville Landless in London walk past an "unfinished and undeveloped railway station" (p. 137). Even the physical appearance of the young brother and sister—Neville and Helena Landless—is said to contain "an indefinable kind of pause . . . equally likened to the pause before a crouch, or a bound" (p. 38). All of these pauses underscore the novel's thematic concern with man's situation in any single moment of time, where he wishes the future to offer great promise but is also aware that the past may become, in the words of the novel's narrator, a great network of "chains that are forever forging, day and night, in the vast ironworks of time and circumstance . . ." (p. 103).

Thackeray's unfinished novel also is concerned with a desire for great futures in relationship to a sense of the "chains" of the past. Even though the point of view of the narrative provides some clues to the plot's final resolution, the possible roads that could be traveled to that end allow the reader to share the characters' sense of anticipation about the future. Although Agnes is at the moment of narration "moored in our harbour of rest, after life's chequered voyage" (p. 271), the reader is frequently in doubt about what immediate event awaits the characters in the action of the novel. Denis's progress in life, for instance, must be along one of many paths often represented by the variety of company he meets as a child: "Seafaring men, speaking a jargon of English, French, Dutch, were constantly dropping in upon us. Dear Heaven! when I think in what a company I have lived, and what a *galère* I rowed in, is it not a wonder that I did not finish where some of my friends did?" (p. 288). The image of chains used by Dickens to suggest the power of the past over the future is also employed by Thackeray. Duval speaks in ominous tones of "that mysterious chain of destiny which was binding *all* these people—me the boy of seven years old; yonder little speechless infant of as many months [Agnes]; that poor wondering lady bereft of reason [Clarisse]; that dark inscrutable companion of hers who brought evil with him wherever he came [de la Motte]" (p. 285).

It is not only the characters in these novels who wish to keep the future open, however; the authors constructing the works seem to insist that their readers benefit from an unpredictable future as well. That is, the form of the Victorian novel embodies the idea of open-endedness. Thackeray's audience learns to complete the frequent unfinished constructions and, in doing so, to piece together key elements of the novel's plot. For example, Dr. Barnard confronts Denis's grandfather in the April 1864 installment with this statement:

> "I know you to be . . ." and the docter whispered something into grandfather's ear, and stalked away.
>   Can you guess by what name the doctor called my grandfather. If he called him hypocrite, *ma foi,* he was not far from wrong. But the truth is, he called him smuggler, and that was a name which fitted hundreds of people along our coast, I promise you. (P. 399)

That "hypocrite" is an accurate but not correct completion of this thought suggests that "smuggler" may also not cover all the possibilities. The final note of the novel's third chapter (and the first installment) also leaves to the reader the task of articulating a character's judgment and more. Agnes's father lies dying from his duel with de la Motte, only then able to state openly what he believes about the Chevalier: "The Comte de Saverne seemed to be about to speak. He lifted himself from the sand, supporting himself on one arm: but all he said was,—You, you—and a great issue of blood rushed from his throat, and he fell back, and, with a few convulsions, died" (p. 291). What each reader feels Agnes's father would have said represents his understanding of this character and de la Motte, though the great gush of blood suggests no words could convey all the human feeling involved in this scene. Thackeray's technique in *Denis Duval,* then, often leaves summations of crucial matters in the plot, like de Saverne's sentence, unfinished.

In Dickens's *Drood,* in addition to the many pauses that stress the theme of an open future, there are pauses in the text that create

140

specific expectations that seem deliberately unresolved, as if Dickens too were resisting in his writing the creation of what he called the "chains" that are "gifted with invincible force to hold and drag" (p. 103)—that is, the events of the past which shape the future. Jasper, for instance, at one point begins a yawn whose natural completion is frustrated. He has been listening to a boring talk by Mr. Sapsea: "Mr. Jasper, in the act of yawning behind his wineglass, puts down that screen and calls up a look of interest. It is a little impaired in its expressiveness by his having a shut-up gape still to dispose of, with watering eyes" (p. 23). As we read this and related descriptions of actions whose natural completions are thwarted, a curious reinforcement of the theme of pauses in the novel occurs. There is again a sense of things continually opening out, but never closing off, of ongoing anticipation that dissipates or disappears rather than is fulfilled.

In the same conversation in which Jasper's yawn begins but does not end, the self-satisfied Sapsea tells of his wife's inability to complete an enthusiastic endorsement of his greatness; "When I made my proposal," says Sapsea, "she did me the honor to be so overshadowed with a species of Awe, as to be able to articulate only the two words, 'O Thou!'—meaning myself. . . . she never could, and she never did, find a phrase satisfactory to her perhaps-too-favourable estimate of my intellect. To the very last . . . she addressed me in the same unfinished terms" (pp. 23–24). Jasper's response to this narration is yet another unfinished expression: "He now abruptly opens [his eyes], and says, in unison with the deepened voice 'Ah!'—rather as if stopping himself on the extreme verge of adding—'men!'" (p. 24). Jasper creates an expectation of resolution for the term "Ah!"—the added syllable, "men," which would make "Amen!" The completion of Jasper's expression would confirm a relationship to Sapsea and his tale—that of the devoted listener. When the expected resolution in *not* provided in Jasper's subsequent speech, Sapsea should reinterpret what his listener has said, arriving at the meaning of "Ah" without "men." In the revised interpretation Jasper acknowledges what Sapsea has said but takes

141

no stand about it; he delivers simply a noncommittal "Ah!" The unthinking Sapsea, however, does not notice the absence of a conclusion to Jasper's phrase, perhaps supplying it unconsciously himself. The readers of the novel *Drood*, however, eventually become aware of the many expectations that are created but never resolved in the text.

Continually shifting, often disappointed expectations are a significant part of response to much Victorian fiction. The creation of unfulfilled expectations is a feature of Dickens's and Thackeray's plots that tends to be ignored by a literary theory stressing the importance of endings in the creation of meaning. The novel Anthony Trollope was working on at his death, *The Landleaguers*, remains like *Drood* and *Duval* unfinished and possesses a similar emphasis on multiple possibilities of development. One of the key elements of Trollope's plot, for instance, is a love story featuring Edith Jones, daughter of an Irish landlord threatened by an organization of Irish peasants—the "Landleague" of the novel's title. This love story, in an uncompleted form like *Drood*'s and *Duval*'s, still features an amusing image of the Victorian need to keep an acceptable future in view.

Captain Yorke Clayton is assigned to protect Mr. Jones, the property owner, during a time when his Irish community is boycotting him and his family. Edith's sister, Ada, manages to fall in love—or to recognize that she has fallen in love—with the captain before Edith does. Ada says to Yorke coyly at one point that he must watch out for his own life in these dangerous times so that he will survive to please "the wife that is to be."[20] Yorke replies that he cannot neglect his duties for what he terms "a cloudy wife" (2:93). Of course, we readers of the novel are encouraged to fill in this "cloudy wife" with the form of Edith or Ada (we cannot be sure which yet). That is, we, like Ada, a character in the novel, are building images for the future, creating a "wife to be."

Ada actually appears the more likely future wife for Clayton because Edith claims, "I mean eventually to take to women's rights, and to make myself generally odious" (2:144). Edith even attempts to further a match between her sister Ada and Yorke; but it is Edith our hero falls for, surprising her with a sudden declaration of love. In a melancholy scene Ada must erase the image of her own romantic future. Whenever Clayton visits the Jones's household, the sisters perform the duties of servants because of the boycott against their family. While "laying her hand upon the pillow" of Clayton's bed, which "her own hands had prepared for him" (2:243), Ada laments that he "cares nothing for me" (2:242) and says that Edith "will be his wife" (2:243). Ada then "turned round upon the bed, and hid her face for a few minutes upon the pillow" (2:243). The following passage sums up her romantic life, replacing a full future of married bliss with the narrow vision of Victorian spinsterhood: "Then she did obliterate the traces of her form which her figure had made upon the bed, and smoothed the pillow, and wiped away the mark of her tear which had fallen on it" (2:244). For only a moment she had become Mrs. Yorke Clayton, the "cloudy wife" of "the hero of her pillow" (3:133).

The Victorian novel seems to feature such moments where character and reader look to the future, building images (of "cloudy wives"), even though many of these imagined futures are never realized (only Ada's form on the bed approaches marriage). Characters and author prefer to be at a moment of potential (a pause) rather than to find themselves fixed in an undesired course by an unrelenting past. There are several small texts within the larger texts of both *Drood* and *Denis Duval* that illustrate further how the Victorian reader's expectations, while not resolved, are nevertheless clearly solicited by their texts' many pauses. Readers, that is, are encouraged at some points almost literally to write their own texts of the novel's many possible futures.

Thackeray in *Denis Duval* describes a character trying to chart a possible course for the future by writing a letter. Clarisse writes Denis's mother that the task of corresponding with her husband (who is away at war) is impossible: "When I write to him, I sit for hours before the paper" (p. 271). No shared future with her husband can be imagined. However, thinking of other possible futures comes easily for Clarisse: "Whereas when I write to you [Denis's mother], my pen runs—runs! . . . So it is when I write to. . . ." (p.

143

271) With another of his unfinished sentences (we add "de la Motte" to the end), Thackeray encourages his readers to write the novel's future. Clarisse's husband also finds an uncompleted text when he returns home from Corsica: "Amongst torn papers and chiffons, in her ladyship's bureau, there was a scrap with one line in her handwriting. '*Ursule, Ursule, le tyran rev.* . . . .' and no more" (p. 279). Just as de Saverne can complete his wife's note ("before two hours were passed he was on horseback, making the first stage of that long journey [to England]!" [p. 279]), so too does Thackeray's audience.

Dickens's narrator in *Drood* also gives his reader open encouragement for such speculation. When Jasper proceeds to a late night meeting with Durdles, for instance, the narrator comments: "Curious, to make a guess [at] the next two people destined to die in Cloisterham" (p. 89). Such an attempt at foresight is demonstrated by the guiding figure of the novel, Mr. Grewgious. When the young Edwin Drood seems unsure of his commitment to Rosa, Grewgious moves into the "blank silence" (p. 81) of Edwin's thoughts about the future. Edwin falls into one of those "pauses" that "come upon us when we have performed any small social rite" (Grewgious had been toasting Rosa as Edwin's fiancée). Unable to project a satisfactory future based on his feelings for Rosa, Edwin falls silent and allows Grewgious to "draw a picture of a true lover's state of mind, tonight" (p. 81). The picture of the future Grewgious presents, it turns out, only emphasizes the fact that Edwin does *not* feel like a "true lover"; realizing that his expectations do not match Grewgious's text, Edwin begins that process of self-examination which leads to the breaking of his engagement to Rosa.

Mr. Grewgious provides another example of looking to the future when he talks with the young heroine of the novel, and in this instance, as was the case several times in *Duval*, a written text underscores the audience's task in reading. Taking a "pocket-book from his coat pocket, and a stump of black-lead pencil from his waistcoat pocket" (p. 58), he ticks off the facts of Rosa's present situation in order to inspire considerations of her future: "I made a

144

guiding memorandum or so—as I usually do, for I have no conversational powers whatever—to which I will, with your persmission, my dear, refer. 'Well and happy.' Truly. You are well and happy, my dear? You look so" (p. 58). Mr. Grewgious's suggesting various descriptive phrases for Rosa's state of mind is parallel to his portrayal of Edwin as lover. And Rosa too finds herself unable to see the same future for herself that Grewgious projects, and so she begins a process of self-examination and revision. The guardian's speculation, image building, both for Edwin and Rosa, then, exists as a model for one of the reader's key functions in Dickens's novel—projecting possible futures for the fiction's characters. At any of the novel's "pauses," the reader inevitably weighs the chances for future events, considers the options available to all of the characters.

Other brief texts in *Duval* develop the notion that the novel reader can decipher signs to reinterpret the past as well as to foresee the future. As he writes, Denis frequently takes out documents concerning his own past: "I take out from my secretary that letter [in which the Count de Saverne called M. de la Motte to a duel], in its tawny ink of fifty years' date, and read it with a strange interest always" (p. 286). Yet each time he reviews such documents "in his arm-chair" years later (p. 391), he is seeing their importance and their relationship to the shape of his life more clearly than ever before. He comments at one point: "the past comes back to me—the stormy past, the strange unhappy yet happy past—and I look at it scared and astonished sometimes; as huntsmen look at the gaps and ditches over which they have leapt, and wonder how they are alive" (p. 391). The "gaps" and "ditches" in Thackeray's narrative, its uncompleted sentences and other omissions, are bridged over by his readers as they gather and interpret additional information in reading. Interestingly, the past's final shape is, in this sense, always ahead of us in reading.

Dickens too includes texts that are interpreted to discover the past. Over the portal of Grewgious's chambers in London are the letters "P J T" and the date "1747." While no authoritative reading of this text of letters is ever provided, the narrator seems to enjoy trying out various possibilities: "it might mean Perhaps John

145

Thomas, or Perhaps Joe Tyler," says the narrator initially (p. 76). Later, he observes, "If P. J. T. in seventeen-forty-seven, or in any other year of his period, drank such wines [as Grewgious provides for his guests]—then, for a certainty, P. J. T. was Pretty Jolly Too" (p. 80). And then, describing Grewgious's private memories of his love for Rosa's mother many years ago, the narrator observes that "there are such unexplored romantic nooks in the unlikeliest men, that even old tinderous and touch-woody P. J. T. Possibly Jabbered Thus, at some odd times, in or about seventeen-forty-seven" (p. 85). Just as Grewgious hopes for the eventual production of his unusual clerk Bazzard's play—"May! . . . May! . . . May! . . . May it come out at last!" (p. 81)—so the reader looks back over what he has read and forward to what he will read in the text of *Drood*, reshaping a past and anticipating many futures.

That readers enjoyed both predicting what might happen and reviewing what had happened in a serial novel is again underscored in Victorian periodical reaction to Thackeray's *Denis Duval* and Dickens's *Drood*.[21] The *Weekly Times* (10 April 1864) specifically recalls (or recommends) for its readers the plot of Thackeray's ongoing serial, stressing "the affecting story of the Countess de Saverne" (p. 2). The *Guardian* on the same date draws attention to the central incident of the second installment: "The hero of the tale, the son of a French barber at Rye, has been taken by his patron to London, and fires a toy-pistol loaded with small shot in the eyes of a highwayman" (p. 338). The common practice of reprinting key passages, often more than a page in length, from the current installment is one way of reviewing a novel's past, as this comment about *Drood* from the *Examiner* shows: "The second number of *The Mystery of Edwin Drood* carries us further into mystery, while it gives a little more individuality to the characters. We are introduced to some fresh *dramatis personae*, one of which, rejoicing in the paradoxical title of Honeythunder, is a true Dickensian impersonation. We regret space will not allow us to quote more than the following. . . ."[22] Other reviews often included detailed summaries. For instance, *Lloyd's Weekly London Newspaper* comments, "By this time the reading public is acquainted with Durdles, the stonemason;

146

with Sapsea, the auctioneer; with Edwin Drood, the young lover; and his betrothed, Miss Rosa Bud—so universal is the appreciation of Dickens."[23]

Looking forward is at least as intriguing as looking back for most Victorian readers, as this comment from *Bell's Weekly Messenger* shows: "Such a commencement as 'The Mystery of Edwin Drood' presents, makes us—as it will do tens of thousands of readers—long for the next month, when a further development of plot, and illustration of character, will be expected."[24] In the serial format, the reader often had picture as well as text by which to interpret the future, as the *News of the World* observes: ". . . the reader will find himself assisted to a solution [of the "mystery" of *Edwin Drood*] by the vignettes on the cover, which, unlike the almanac hieroglyphics really foretel [sic] what is going to happen."[25] Because the story has not ended for these serial readers in the midst of the text, predictions about the future are a more important part of their literary experience than they could be for later readers of single volume editions, as this comment from the *Academy* suggests: "But Dickens was never very particular as to the possibility of the means by which his characters were made happy towards the last number, and for aught we can tell to the contrary, half-a-dozen principal contributors to the dénoument may have remained uninvented when the work was cut short in the middle."[26]

Although Victorian readers may not have been able to chart in advance exact, complete paths to the resolutions of their serial tales, they could be confident that there was a method in such storytelling. The narrator of Dickens's novel observes at one point that his is a story with relentless forward motion, which "will itself unfold as it advances" (p. 12) a logic for its sometimes indirect style. Thackeray's narrative too is said to be full of "zig-zag journeys" (p. 391), deliberately creating uncertainty about the future. The unique styles of both novels, with their different indirections, include key pauses where the reader, like the characters, is building images of past and future. It is, however, not only within the text, in its narrative pauses, that these Victorian authors offer their readers the chance to fashion an ever-changing version of the past and a whole range of

147

possible futures. Between installments of these serial novels, in the month-long pauses, the original Victorian reader was perhaps most free to "prefigure possible horizons" (to return to Iser's terms).[27]

Each installment of Thackeray's *Denis Duval* involves ambiguity about the novel's future.[28] Although the Count de Saverne's death comes neatly at the end of the first installment in *Cornhill*, a host of questions remain about what is in store for de la Motte (his killer), Agnes (his daughter), and Denis himself. The second installment features the young hero's unexpected shooting of a highwayman, which makes him the enemy of Joseph Weston, with whose family Agnes is staying. Thus, how hero and heroine are to get together again in the next issue, with Joseph "waiting with a horse-whip" (p. 408) for Denis, becomes a matter of uncertainty. The third install-ment ends with the news that "we were at war with France" (p. 535) and the French Catholic Agnes worrying that Denis Duval might become "my enemy" (p. 536). Denis's career at sea is just beginning at the end of the fourth installment as he finds himself suddenly involved in war: "Then came a broadside from us—the first I had ever heard in battle" (p. 654). Where he will travel and what dangers he must face before his return to England occupy the thoughts of readers anticipating the next installment.

The pauses between installments of *Drood* are also dominated by questions about what has happened and what will happen that characters and readers attempt to answer. After a late-night, myste-rious conversation with Durdles in number 1, for example, Jasper strikes a thoughtful pose in his room. His pipe smoke at the very end of the installment recalls the opium smoke that opened the novel. The last sentence of the number invites the reader to a spec-ulation like Jasper's: "His nephew [Edwin] lies asleep, calm and untroubled. John Jasper stands looking down upon him, his un-lighted pipe in his hand, for some time, with a fixed and deep attention. Then, hushing his footsteps, he passes to his own room, lights his pipe, and delivers himself to the Spectres it invokes at midnight" (p. 32). Number 2 also ends suggestively, with a ques-tion. The fatherly Grewgious had said of the two young characters

Edwin and Rosa, "God bless them both!" while Jasper replied, "God save them both!" (p. 64). When Grewgious notes the change, Jasper inquires, "Is there any difference?" (p. 64), causing *us* to wonder at the distinction. Number 3 closes with what is termed an "unaccountable sort of expedition" (p. 89) among the tombs and crypts beneath the Cloisterham cathedral. Although the tour taken by Jaspers, Durdles, and the inexplicable Deputy ends with this installment, the narrator encourages us to wonder about the need for more such unexplained events when he adds that it "comes to an end—for the time" (p. 96). Jasper's diary entry concludes number 4. Calling Edwin's absence a "mystery," he vows to "devote [himself] to his [murderer's] destruction" (p. 128), raising questions about Jasper's charges and his own motives. Number 5 ends with yet another ominous note, as the young heroine, Rosa, though under Grewgious's care in London, looks as if she is "a dove in a high roost in a cage of lions" (p. 160) that "might tumble out." Left consistently at the end of each number with questions or speculations about past and future, then, the reader has a month to pursue alternative versions of the lives of Dickens's fictional characters. These image-building readers found considerable freedom in each of those thirty-day gaps to plot a number of possible courses for all the people of Dickens's imagined world.

The Victorian author and reader's looking ahead, both for more of one text and for more new texts, underscores a basic optimism, a confidence both that enough of the potential of the moment will be realized in the future and that the creative activity of speculation is itself worthwhile. As Ina Ferris writes, "From the temporary endings achieved at the close of each serial number to the proliferation of novel series, nineteenth-century fiction continually closes only in order to open, concludes only in order to continue."[29] This nineteenth-century optimism is revealed not only in the theme of openness found in *Denis Duval*, *Drood*, and *The Landleaguers;* it is clearly seen in the responses to the novels recorded in the popular periodical press. The Victorian audience automatically assumes the potential of the stories told by its major authors. The *Saturday Review,*

149

for example, automatically assumes that "*The Landleaguers* would evidently, if [Trollope] had been able to finish it, have done no discredit to him. . . ."[30]

The *Examiner* on 2 January 1864 expresses a similar assurance about Thackeray's soon-to-be-published tale: ". . . at the time of his death he was engaged on a work of fiction which is spoken very highly of by those to whom the earlier sheets were shown" (p. 9). This Victorian faith in their major writers' creative power was not misplaced in Thackeray's case according to many modern critics. Gordon Ray, *Thackeray: the Age of Wisdom* (New York: McGraw-Hill, 1958), for instance, calls *Denis Duval* "a magnificent fragment" (p. 411) and notes Thackeray's energy of composition at the end of his life: "Much action is packed into the three and a half numbers which Thackeray wrote, but far more was planned for those which remained" (p. 409). J. A. Sutherland, *Thackeray at Work* (London: Athlone Press, 1974), argues that *Duval* "promises in fact a recovery in age of the powers of youth" (p. 110). And Robert A. Colby, *Thackeray's Canvass of Humanity: An Author and His Public* (Columbus: Ohio State Univ. Press, 1979), says, "Thackeray's half-told tale, in its incisiveness, dramatic sweep, and narrative drive, reveals his mastery purely as a literary artist, if not his full intellectual strength" (p. 448).

A number of papers reviewing the beginnings of new serials specifically use the word "promise" in articulating this Victorian desire for potentiality. The editor of *Cornhill*, Frederick Greenwood, said that the last installment of *Duval* was "blooming with new promise like the apple trees in this month of May."[31] *Bell's Weekly Messenger* comments, "Indeed, during the whole of Mr. Dickens's literary career, we may in truth say we do not remember ever to have read the first number of any one of his works which manifested anything like the promise which 'The Mystery of Edwin Drood' indicates."[32] Similarly, the *Illustrated Times* observes, ". . . if one may judge by the first installment, 'Edwin Drood' promises to be one of Mr. Dickens's happiest efforts."[33] And the *Examiner* observes, "When Mr. Charles Dickens lately bade farewell as a public reader, he informed us that his pen would not rust in inglorious idleness. We have a redemption of his promise in the issue of the first number of a new tale, 'The Mystery of Edwin Drood.' . . . The story is not sufficiently advanced to enable us to form an idea of the plot, but it promises to be fully equal to anything the author has already written."[34] In an even more specific prediction of fulfillment, the *Athenaeum* refers to "that exquisitely promising Rosa Bud" and "her equally promising affianced lover."[35]

The Victorian audience's insistence on promise in their lives and in their works of art in part accounts for the persistent emphasis on their authors' creativity. The prolificacy of Victorian writers is consistently remarked, particularly when the authors reach the ends of their careers. The *Athenaeum* claims that *The Landleaguers* "shows no falling off in Mr. Trollope's peculiar power."[36] Thackeray's gifts seem to survive the grave in the *Guardian's* comment: "The Spirit of Mr. Thackeray still continues to linger around the *The Cornhill Magazine* in his characteristic story called 'Denis Duval,' the scene of which is laid in the early days of George III."[37] The *Press* sounds a frequently heard note: in *Denis Duval* Thackeray demonstrated a final time that his creative powers had never slackened and that he was "very careful and studious . . . in the construction of his works" even near his death.[38] It is, of course, Dickens's vitality and energy that are most celebrated in the Victorian periodical press. The *Spectator,* for instance, identifies ". . . the great intellectual mystery of Dickens's fertile genius" as a "power of reduplicating a single humorous conception of character into an elaborate structure of strictly analagous conceptions" or an "inexhaustible power of illustrating" character.[39] The same article finds his characters as alive as their author, "full to overflowing of fresh vitality and infinite humor."[40]

This concentration on the creative powers of authors fits the Victorian age with its many expanding horizons in science, education, politics, commerce, and industry. Victorians had to believe in their own generative power in such a rapidly changing and growing scene. Their relentless optimism about the future created their only real security. Unfinished fragments or installments of novels belonged in such a worldview where ends were remote enough as to

151

be almost unnecessary. Wherever they were in the middles of texts, Victorians concentrated on the multiple potentials of that single moment in time. In our own century, of course, as Jerome Beaty has shown, we fear the fragments that lie around us and offer no hope of fulfillment.[41] From this lack of faith in the future we derive at least a part of our aesthetic insistence that art remain whole. We argue that our fictions must possess an organic unity when life does not. Victorians could stand their "loose baggy monsters" of fiction because the audience reading them was itself whole in ways no modern audience has been.

This sense of ongoing process in the literary world is further revealed in periodical reaction to Victorian fiction. In the same months that the final numbers of Dickens's *Edwin Drood* are reviewed by the weekly press, for instance, there is consistent reference to new fiction, in a sense, picking up where Dickens leaves off. Dickens's death suggests the end of an era to many like the *Examiner:* "Another place is vacant in the ranks of great writers, and the ranks must be closed in; for who from the rear line shall step forward to fill the void?"[42] But the beginning of the next age of fiction is evident at the same time in the commencement of new serial fiction of a different kind, as the *Weekly Times* observes: "The *Cornhill* gives, this month, a well-selected variety of good reading matter. [The first chapters of George Meredith's] 'The Adventures of Harry Richmond' are decidedly interesting, and somewhat new in treatment."[43] The *Illustrated Times* also notes the new work, which departs from some mid-Victorian conventions: "What a splendid number is the *Cornhill!* 'Harry Richmond,' though a little strained and fantastic, is full of life and poetic humour."[44]

This argument about the qualities of unfinished novels that appealed to Victorian readers, however, also suggests a changing critical climate in the postmodern world. The critical approach of Wolfgang Iser isolates a factor in the reading experience that has its attraction for many contemporary readers. Thackeray's critics are showing new interest in *Denis Duval. Drood* continues to be published (even rewritten) and read today. And *The Landleaguers* has been reissued as recently as 1981. This contemporary interest in unfinished novels suggests that readers in our own time enjoy not only an author's ability to construct a lasting work of art satisfying a need for order; we appreciate as well the chances in reading to be free, to be in the midst of some process, keeping open a sense of possibility that may or may not be present in real life. The period of literary criticism that celebrated the ideals of appropriate form and autonomous texts is drawing to a close and making possible a rediscovery of great works of art whose features are best revealed in different theoretical perspectives, perspectives that allow us to explore the middles of texts, the space between the numbers in serial fiction.

Thackeray's achievements are especially impressive in this regard; the middles of his novels generated profound effects on his Victorian readers. Focusing his audience's concern with genealogy in *Henry Esmond,* for instance, he systematically broadened and deepened their understanding of the relationships of family history and national events. As far-reaching, however, and less fully recognized in contemporary criticism are Thackeray's uses of the serial form, the nearly two-year length of the reading experience. He developed his characters like Amelia Sedley not only in the text of *Vanity Fair* but also in the context that surrounded its original reading, England's midcentury complacency with its position in the world and its citizens' assumed courage in facing adversity. Further, using the several years' time frame of publication in *Pendennis,* he extended the audience's sense of growth and development in a literary experience, expanding the favorite nineteenth-century form of the bildungsroman. Responding to a debate in his society about the literary profession, Thackeray also worked to educate his "actual" reading public by positing in his continuing story about a writer's career an "ideal" reader who appreciates literary effort. And Thackeray underscored the Victorian theme of separation when telling an "old story" of meetings and partings by using a publication format that made audience, author, and fictional company come together and break apart twenty-three times during the course of reading his novel.

Looking again at the middles of these long Victorian novels— and at moments in the middle of the history of the novel as a genre—may now show us new things about nineteenth-century

153

consciousness. Studying the unfinished novel of Thackeray, along with those by Dickens and Trollope, suggests that Victorian audiences found their identity (a profound faith in the future) in the process of reading, not in its aftermath—reading Thackeray, not Thackeray. The texts of Victorian novels, with their insistence on ever-expanding horizons, counted on and furthered their readers' belief in progress. Without faith in the ultimate outcome of history, modernists have found long nineteenth-century novels unfulfilling. Whole audiences can read literary pieces; but fragmented readers prefer the "organic whole" of a completed text. New readers of the novel, however, may now be ready, in the middles of texts, to pause, to remain poised at the moment of building images. As nineteenth-century audiences learned by reading Thackeray in this way, we in the twentieth century can reread Thackeray to recover both the range of his great art and its involvement in fundamental elements of Victorian culture.

Notes

Abbreviations

EIC	*Essays in Criticism*
ELH	*Journal of English Literary History*
MP	*Modern Philology*
NCF	*Nineteenth-Century Fiction*
NLH	*New Literary History*
PMLA	*Publications of the Modern Language Association of America*
SEL	*Studies in English Literature, 1500–1900*
SNNTS	*Studies in the Novel*
VNL	*Victorian Newsletter*
VPR	*Victorian Periodicals Review*
VS	*Victorian Studies*

Chapter 1

1. Wayne Booth, *The Rhetoric of Fiction* (Chicago: Univ. of Chicago Press, 1961); Wolfgang Iser, *The Implied Reader: Patterns of Communication in Prose Fiction from Bunyan to Beckett* (Baltimore: Johns Hopkins Univ. Press, 1974); Walter Slatoff, *With Respect to Readers* (Ithaca: Cornell Univ. Press); David Bleich, *Readings and Feelings: An Introduction to Subjective Criticism* (Urbana: National Council of Teachers of English, 1975), pp. 20–21. This statement is italicized.

2. Norman Holland, *Five Readers Reading* (New Haven: Yale Univ. Press, 1975), p. 40. This statement is italicized.

3. Stanley Fish, "Literature in the Reader: Affective Stylistics," in *Self-Consuming Artifacts: The Experience of Seventeenth-Century Literature*, by Stanley Fish (Berkeley: Univ. of California Press, 1972), p. 399. The essay first appeared in *New Literary History* 2 (Autumn 1970): 123–62.

4. Among the many helpful studies of form, see Edgar F. Harden, "The Discipline and Significance of Form in *Vanity Fair*," *PMLA* 82 (December 1967): 530–42; John

Loofbourow, *Thackeray and the Form of Fiction* (Princeton: Princeton Univ. Press, 1964); Juliet McMaster, *Thackeray: The Major Novels* (Toronto: Univ. of Toronto Press, 1971); Bernard J. Paris, "The Psychic Structure of *Vanity Fair*," *Victorian Studies* 10 (June 1967): 389–410; J. A. Sutherland, *Thackeray at Work* (London: Athlone Press, 1974); Kathleen Tillotson, *Novels of the Eighteen-Forties* (London: Oxford Univ. Press, 1954).

5. Iser, *Implied Reader*, p. 106: "empty spaces [in the narrative] are bound to occur, spurring the reader's imagination to detect the assumption which might have motivated the narrator's attitude." See also G. Armour Craig, "On the Style of *Vanity Fair*," in *Twentieth Century Interpretations of Vanity Fair*, edited by M. G. Sundell (Englewood Cliffs, N.J.: Prentice-Hall, 1969), p. 72: "[Thackeray] could not be clear without being untruthful, and he could not be truthful without being obscure"; and McMaster, *Thackeray: The Major Novels*, p. 9: "The reader has to be prepared to make his own independent judgment just as much in the passages of commentary as in the passages of direct scenic presentation, and frequently more so, because of the deceptive plausibility of the commentator's arguments."

6. For an excellent summary of critical approaches to Becky, see John H. Hagan, "*Vanity Fair*: Becky Brought to Book Again," *Studies in the Novel* 7 (Winter 1975): 479–506.

7. Iser, *Implied Reader*, p. 118: "The reader is offered a host of different perspectives, and so is almost continually confronted with the problem of how to make them consistent." See also U. C. Knoepflmacher, *Laughter and Despair: Readings in Ten Novels of the Victorian Era* (Berkeley: Univ. of California Press, 1971), pp. 50–83, and McMaster, *Thackeray: The Major Novels*, pp. 1–49.

8. William Makepeace Thackeray, *Vanity Fair*, edited by Geoffrey and Kathleen Tillotson (Boston: Houghton Mifflin Co., Riverside Edition, 1963), pp. 23–24. Subsequent references will be to this edition, which reflects the original parts' divisions, and will include pagination in the text. The Tillotsons' introduction also provides helpful insight into the novel's composition.

9. Jack P. Rawlins, *Thackeray's Novels: A Fiction That Is True* (Berkeley: Univ. of California Press, 1974), pp. 1–35; 234–36. See also Iser, *Implied Reader*, p. 119: "Thus, instead of society, the reader finds himself to be the object of criticism."

10. This description appears in "Before the Curtain," printed as a preface to the first volume edition, though Thackeray wrote it after the novel was completed and it appeared first as part of the final installment in July 1848. For a history of Becky's appeal, see John H. Hagan, "Becky Brought to Book Again," who refutes all those who have suggested Becky deserves the admiration she inspires.

11. Stanley Fish, *Surprised by Sin: The Reader in Paradise Lost* (Berkeley: Univ. of California Press, 1971), p. 344. That Thackeray borrowed more than a title from Bunyan seems clear, particularly if Fish is correct when he argues that altering the reader's perspective is the narrative's primary goal in *The Pilgrim's Progress* (*Self-Consuming Artifacts*, pp. 224–64). Loofbourow notes this similarity between Milton and Thackeray: "One of the ironies of literature is that Becky's heroic adventures have been taken . . . seriously. . . . it is the same response that once made Satan the hero of *Paradise Lost*" (*Thackeray and the Form of Fiction*, p. 26).

12. An example of the traditional dismissal of Amelia as uninteresting (or worse) is Dorothy Van Ghent, *The English Novel: Form and Function* (1953; reprint, New York:

Harper & Row, 1967), p. 176, who says that "beside [Becky] there is room and meaning for Amelia only as a victim." A. E. Dyson, "*Vanity Fair:* An Irony against Heroes," in *Twentieth Century Interpretations,* p. 87, however, argues that Amelia's "characterization is at least as subtle as Becky's," and Bernard J. Paris, "Psychic Structure of *Vanity Fair,*" p. 410, agrees: "Critics who regard Amelia and Dobbin as puppets have failed to appreciate the complexity of their characterization. . . ." Juliet McMaster, *Thackeray: The Major Novels,* pp. 92–96, and Katharine M. Rogers, "A Defense of Thackeray's Amelia," *Texas Studies in Literature and Language* 11 (1970): 1,367–74, have furthered a revaluation of Amelia's role in the novel.

13. This omission has been noted, but not explored, by several critics. Dyson, "An Irony against Heroes," p. 74, observes that "we are never shown Amelia's deepest moments of grief, though we know the torment they must be." In another context, Barbara Hardy, *The Exposure of Luxury: Radical Themes in Thackeray* (Pittsburgh: Univ. of Pittsburgh Press, 1972), p. 35, notes one place where Thackeray "leaves the narrative of [Amelia's] feelings incomplete."

14. Juliet McMaster is particularly insightful in her discussion of Thackeray's handling of serial publication, noting that the novel's "continuous fabric of existence goes on, over months or years, with its dramas and disappointments but without resolution, for the novel's characters outside the novel" (*Thackeray: The Major Novels,* p. 24), the central concept I attempt to develop here. See also James M. Keech, "'. . . Make 'em Wait': Installment Suspense in Thackeray's *Vanity Fair,*" *Serif* 3 (1966): 9–12.

15. Wolfgang Iser, *The Act of Reading: A Theory of Aesthetic Response* (Baltimore: Johns Hopkins Univ. Press, 1978), p. 192.

16. Barbara Hardy, *Exposure of Luxury,* pp. 24–25, has discussed another moment in the novel where the reader's and a character's minds share a single thought, when Rebecca admires Rawdon striking Lord Steyne in chapter 53.

17. Barbara Hardy, *Exposure of Luxury,* p. 57, sums up our relationship to Amelia: "We shall begin by loving her and feeling with her, in her friendship, love, grief, maternal affection, but we shall eventually learn the limitations of sensibility uncontrolled by reason; she will worship her unworthy husband, alive and dead, spoil her son, and make sentimental demands on Dobbin, her patient lover."

18. Fish, *Suprised by Sin,* p. 344, makes the same observation in regard to the reader's relationship to Satan in *Paradise Lost:* "At some point during this sequence of actions the reader becomes immune to the Satanic appeal because he has learned what it is, or to be more precise, what it is not. 'Some point,' however, will be a different point for each reader, depending on the extent to which he is committed to the false ideal Satan exemplifies."

19. *The Letters and Private Papers of William Makepeace Thackeray,* edited by Gordon N. Ray (London: Oxford Univ. Press, 1945), 2:309.

Chapter 2

1. Jerome Buckley, *Season of Youth: The Bildungsroman from Dickens to Golding* (Cambridge: Harvard Univ. Press, 1974), p. 18.

2. Buckley, *Season of Youth,* p. 29. Recent studies of *Pendennis* touching on the development of character include Robert Bledsoe, "*Pendennis* and the Power of Sentimentality," *PMLA* 19 (1976): 871–83; Robert A. Colby, *Thackeray's Canvass of Humanity: An Author*

and His Public (Columbus: Ohio State Univ. Press, 1979); Ina Ferris, "The Demystification of Laura Pendennis," *SNNTS* 13 (Summer 1981): 122–32; and Thomas L. Jeffers, "Thackeray's *Penndennis:* Son and Gentleman," *NCF* 33 (1978): 175–93.

3. Susan R. Suleiman and Inge Crosman, eds., *The Reader in the Text: Essays on Audience and Interpretation* (Princeton: Princeton Univ. Press, 1980), p. 6.

4. *The Reader and the Text,* p. 5.

5. Gordon Ray, *Thackeray: The Age of Wisdom* (New York: McGraw-Hill, 1958); Edgar F. Harden, *The Emergence of Thackeray's Serial Fiction* (Athens: Univ. of Georgia Press, 1979); J. A. Sutherland, *Thackeray at Work* (London: Athlone Press, 1974); and Colby, *Thackeray's Canvass.* Colby demonstrates how *"Pendennis* is best savored in connection with its original circumstances and milieu" (p. 304).

6. The shifting of "form" from its place within the text to a position in the reader's response to a text is one of Stanley Fish's contributions to the current debate. In summarizing the development of reader-oriented criticism, Jane P. Tompkins, in *Reader-Response Criticism: From Formalism to Post-Structuralism,* edited by Jane P. Tompkins (Baltimore: Johns Hopkins Univ. Press, 1980), explains Fish's contention: "Texts are written by readers, not read, since, the argument now states, the formal features of the text, the authorial intentions they are normally taken to represent, and the reader's interpretive strategies are mutually interdependent" (p. xxii).

7. William Makepeace Thackeray, *The History of Pendennis: His Fortunes and Misfortunes, His Friends and His Greatest Enemy* (London: Bradbury & Evans, 1848–50), 2:210. I am citing here the original parts publication, the pagination of which corresponds to the later two-volume edition. Thus, number 13 begins with page 1 of volume 2. Subsequent references to *Pendennis* will be made in the text and will include volume and page numbers in parentheses. For a detailed history of *Pendennis*'s publication, see Peter L. Shillingsburg, "Thackeray's *Pendennis* in America," *Papers of the Bibliographical Society of America* 68 (1974): 325–29.

8. Buckley, *Season of Youth,* p. 22.

9. A preface appeared at the end of the final double number, and in later editions it is usually included at the beginning of the novel. For further analyses of Thackeray's narrative technique in this novel, see Edgar F. Harden, "Theatricality in *Pendennis," Ariel* 4 (1973): 74–94; Barbara Hardy, *The Exposure of Luxury: Radical Themes in Thackeray* (Pittsburgh: Univ. of Pittsburgh Press, 1972), pp. 37–45; and Juliet McMaster, *Thackeray: The Major Novels* (Toronto: Univ. of Toronto Press, 1971), pp. 51–86.

10. Jean Sudrann, " 'The Philosopher's Property': Thackeray and the Use of Time," *VS* 10 (1967): 365.

11. Sudrann, " 'The Philosopher's Property,' " 369.

12. W. J. Harvey, *Character and the Novel* (Ithaca: Cornell Univ. Press, 1965), p. 110. Harvey underestimates, I think, the effect of serialization on the reception a novel might enjoy, calling it only "a minor point" (p. 111); but his observations about the form have given me considerable direction in this study.

13. Martin Fido, *"The History of Pendennis:* A Reconsideration," *EIC* 14 (1964): 363–79, also discusses the reader's coming to find out who Laura is in the first two numbers of the novel. James H. Wheatley, *Patterns in Thackeray's Fiction* (Cambridge, Mass.: MIT Press, 1969), has justly praised *Pendennis*'s first two numbers as "a unit as controlled and sustained as anything he ever wrote" (p. 135). Another conspicuous example of the flashback tech-

nique occurs in number 9, where Altamont/Amory confronts his daughter, Betsy/Blanche. Before Amory has the chance to reveal his identity, the sound of disturbance in the nearby ballroom distracts these characters *and* the narrator. Thackeray then backs up the narrative to account for the noise of the confrontation between Pen and Miroblant.

14. Wolfgang Iser, *The Act of Reading: A Theory of Aesthetic Response* (Baltimore: Johns Hopkins Univ. Press, 1978), pp. 128–29.

15. I have made the same point, more briefly, in reference to *David Copperfield* in "Clocking the Reader in the Long Victorian Novel," *VNL*, no. 59 (Spring 1981): 22–25.

16. For other aspects of Thackeray's composition, see Edgar F. Harden, "The Serial Structure of Thackeray's *Pendennis*," *Revue de l'Université d'Ottawa* 45 (1974): 167–80. Wheatley, *Patterns in Thackeray's Fiction*, p. 106, has also drawn attention to the process of Pen's growth as a series of falls that lead to wisdom, but he does not link it to the novel's serial structure. In the introduction to the Penguin *Pendennis* (Baltimore: Penguin Books, 1972), J. I. M. Stewart touches briefly on the effects of installment structure when he observes that the narrator's style in the novel is "welcome whenever he drops in on us (*Pen* dropped in, after all, in monthly parts); and we are quickly led, somehow, to acquiesce in the assumption that just this is what, at the moment, we require of a novel" (p. 10). Robert A. Colby, *Fiction with a Purpose* (Bloomington: Indiana Univ. Press, 1967), pp. 138–77, also discusses some of the effects of serialization, including response to many of the novel's illustrations. At one point, he specifically points to things Victorians "could have been reading in between the installments of *Pen*" (p. 148), which would have also affected the ways in which the audience reacted to the protagonist's growth.

17. Jeffers, "Thackeray's *Pendennis*," p. 185, explains this episode within the context of Pen's sexual development.

18. Such interaction of the reader's world with the world of the fiction as the novel is coming out in installments is an aspect of the literary experience of many nineteenth-century masterpieces that needs further study. A welcome reference tool for such scholarship is J. Don Vann's *Victorian Novels in Serial* (New York: MLA, 1985), which lists the installment novels of sixteen Victorian authors and the parts' divisions for each text. In "Teaching Long Victorian Novels in Parts," *VNL*, no. 58 (Fall, 1980): 29–32, I explore how the extended time frame of a Victorian serial can be copied in the classroom.

19. Peter L. Shillingsburg, "The First Edition of Thackeray's *Pendennis*," *Papers of the Bibliographical Society of America* 66 (1972): 42, points out that a reason behind the demands for reprints of the early numbers "may have been pressure from readers made impatient by the four-month delay in the publication of volume one as a whole, imposed by Thackeray's illness."

20. Ray, *Age of Wisdom*, pp. 113–16 and 136–38. summarizes the dispute.

21. Ray, *Age of Wisdom*, p. 109, notes that "Thackeray's contemporaries found Pen's battle with himself and eventual redemption intensely interesting: to later readers it has seemed increasingly insipid." Although much modern disfavor is a response to Thackeray's treatment of certain issues, complaints like Robert Alan Donovan's that "Thackeray's imaginative vision does not confront life as process, as a continuing movement of development and change" (*The Shaping Vision: Imagination in the English Novel from Defoe to Dickens* [Ithaca: Cornell Univ. Press, 1966], p. 199) seem to me to miss much of the original character of the work.

22. David Masson, "The Literary Profession," *Eclectic Magazine* 21 (November 1850):

364; reprinted from *North British Review* 13 (August 1850). See also the *Literary World,* 16 February 1850, where a reviewer notes that Thackeray's illness "darkened the cheerfulness of club rooms" (p. 151).

Chapter 3

1. Wolfgang Iser, *The Act of Reading: A Theory of Aesthetic Response* (Baltimore: John Hopkins Univ. Press, 1978), p. 34 ("implied" reader); p. 28 ("actual" reader). See also "Indeterminacy and the Reader's Response in Prose Fiction", in *Aspects of Narrative: Selected Papers from the English Institute,* edited by J. Hillis Miller (New York: Columbia Univ. Press, 1971), pp. 14–17.

2. Iser has discussed the installment novel briefly within the context of his theory of the "blank" in literary texts. The blank, according to Iser, "designates a vacancy in the overall system of the text, the filling of which brings about an interaction of textual patterns" (*Act of Reading,* p. 182). The weeks or months between installments in the serial novel can be said to create additional blanks or to accentuate existing blanks (p. 192), where the reader has more opportunity than usual to combine patterns of the text in new formulations. Meir Sternberg, *Expositional Modes and Temporal Ordering in Fiction* (Baltimore: Johns Hopkins Univ. Press, 1978), p. 50, argues that a literary "text may be conceived of as a dynamic system of gaps." In a summary of the critical approach of Pierre Macherey, Terry Eagleton reminds us that one can see much in the gaps or blanks of a text, both what the audience automatically supplies and what the author is unable to say: "It is in the significant silences of a text, in its gaps and absences, that the presence of ideology can be most positively felt. . . . in trying to tell the truth in his own way, for example, the author finds himself forced to reveal the limits of the ideology within which he writes" (*Marxism and Literary Criticism* [Berkeley: Univ. of California Press, 1976], pp. 34–35). For the details of Thackeray's illness, which led to this blank, see Gordon Ray, *Thackeray: The Age of Wisdom* (New York: McGraw-Hill, 1958), pp. 108–26. As Richard Altick explains in great detail in "Varieties of Readers' Response: The Case of *Dombey and Son*" (*Yearbook of English Studies,* 1980), "contemporary reviews" are "the principle source of knowledge" about "readers' response" (p. 75) to Victorian fiction. Reviewers are not, of course, all the original readers, nor are their judgments always the same as most readers; yet, as Altick did in discussing *Dombey and Son* I try to base my generalizations about actual readers on specific contemporary reviews.

3. Few critics have bothered to study the phenomenon of installment reading in this way; but because serial publication was such a dominant mode of the Victorians throughout the century, a new look at its effect on actual readers promises a new understanding of the whole era. An exception is Ian Gregor, ed., *Reading the Victorian Novel: Detail into Form* (New York: Barnes & Noble, 1980). For a study along different lines of audience reaction to the same two serial novels I focus on here, see Rebecca Rodolff, "*The Weekly Chronicle*'s Month-by-Month Reception of *Pendennis* and *David Copperfield,*" *VPR* 14 (Fall 1981): 101–11. See also my own "Clocking the Reader in the Long Victorian Novel", *VNL,* no. 59 (Spring 1981): 22–25.

4. *The Letters and Private Papers of William Makepeace Thackeray,* edited by Gordon N. Ray (London: Oxford Univ. Press, 1945), 2:631.

5. *Letters and Papers of Thackeray,* 2:636. Carl Dawson, *Victorian Noon: English Literature in 1850* (Baltimore: Johns Hopkins Univ. Press, 1979), pp. 153–78, places Thack-

eray's ambivalent feelings about the status of writers within the broad context of Victorian culture in chapter 7, "Men of Letters as Hacks and Heroes." For a detailed study of Dickens's feelings about the author's profession, see Robert L. Patten, *Charles Dickens and His Publishers* (Oxford: Oxford Univ. Press, 1978).

6. R. F. Whale, *Copyright: Evolution, Theory and Practice* (London: Longman, 1971), p. 13.

7. Whale, *Copyright*, p. 24.

8. Whale, *Copyright*, p. 13.

9. J. A. Sutherland, *Victorian Novelists and Publishers* (Chicago: Univ. of Chicago Press, 1976), p. 94.

10. Cited in Victor Bonham-Carter, *Authors by Profession* (London: Society of Authors, 1978), p. 82.

11. Bonham-Carter, *Authors by Profession* p. 83.

12. Bonham-Carter, *Authors by Profession* p. 83.

13. See E. P. Thompson, "Time, Work-Discipline and Industrial Capitalism," in *Essays in Social History,* edited by M. W. Flinn and T. C. Smout (Oxford: Clarendon Press, 1974), pp. 39–77, for an account of the parallel movement among workers.

14. Sutherland, *Victorian Novelists*. p. 85.

15. Walter Besant, who successfully organized the Society of Authors in 1884, explained why authors were unable to work together in 1843: "Authors—the producers of literary property—were still considered as publishers' hacks" (cited in Bonham-Carter, *Authors by Profession,* p. 86).

16. Bonham-Carter, *Authors by Profession,* p. 87.

17. Bonham-Carter, *Authors by Profession,* p. 88.

18. William Makepeace Thackeray, *The History of Pendennis* (London: Bradbury & Evans, 1848–50), 1:31. Pagination in the original parts matches the later two-volume edition.

19. Robert A. Colby, *Thackeray's Canvass of Humanity* (Columbus: Ohio State Univ. Press, 1979), p. 287: "Pendennis and Warrington join various disparate elements of Thackeray's temperament as writer. . . ."

20. *Spectator,* 21 December 1850; reprinted in *Thackeray: The Critical Heritage,* edited by Geoffrey Tillotson and Donald Hawes (London: Routledge & Kegan Paul, 1968), pp. 101–2.

21. "David Copperfield, and Pendennis," *Prospective Review,* May 1851, p. 173.

22. "Thackeray and Dickens," *Literary World,* 7 June 1851, p. 455.

23. Colby, *Thackeray's Canvass,* p. 9.

24. Philip Collins, *Charles Dickens: David Copperfield,* Studies in English Literature, no. 67 (London: Edward Arnold, 1977), pp. 39–40.

25. Maurice Beebe, *Ivory Towers and Sacred Founts: The Artist as Hero in Fiction from Goethe to Joyce* (New York: New York Univ. Press, 1964), p. 88.

26. Philip Collins, ed., *Dickens: The Critical Heritage* (New York: Barnes & Noble, 1971), p. 242.

27. Angus Wilson, *The World of Charles Dickens* (London: Martin Secker & Warburg, 1970), p. 216.

28. *Blackwood's Magazine,* April 1855, p. 461.

29. Charles Dickens, *The Personal History of David Copperfield* (London: Bradbury &

Evans, 1850). Here, and in subsequent references, I include page and date in parentheses in the text.

30. John Forster, *The Life of Charles Dickens* (London: Chapman & Hall, 1872–74), 2:432–62, and 3:1–20. John Butt and Kathleen Tillotson, *Dickens at Work* (London: Methuen & Co., 1957), pp. 114–76.

31. See Forster, *Life of Dickens* 2:432–34.

32. Robert Patten, "Autobiography into Autobiography: The Evolution of *David Copperfield,*" in *Approaches to Victorian Autobiography,* edited by George P. Landow (Athens, Ohio: Ohio Univ. Press, 1979), p. 281.

33. Butt and Tillotson, *Dickens at Work,* pp. 136–45.

34. Butt and Tillotson, *Dickens at Work,* p. 140.

35. Forster, *Life of Dickens* 2:453–54.

36. Beebe, *Ivory Towers,* p. 91. See also Samuel Barnes, "Dickens and Copperfield: The Hero as Man of Letters," in *The Classic British Novel,* edited by Howard M. Harper, Jr., and Charles Edge (Athens, Ga.: Univ. of Georgia Press, 1972), pp. 85–102.

37. "Autobiography into Autobiography," pp. 269–91.

38. Ray, *Age of Wisdom,* p. 108.

39. See Robert L. Patten, "The Fight at the Top of the Tree: *Vanity Fair* versus *Dombey and Son,*" *Studies in English Literature* 10 (1970): 759–73.

40. N. N. Feltes, "To Saunter, To Hurry: Dickens, Time and Industrial Capitalism," *Victorian Studies* 20 (1977): 245–67.

Chapter 4

1. Reprinted in *Thackeray: The Critical Heritage,* edited by Geoffrey Tillotson and Donald Hawes (London: Routledge & Kegan Paul, 1968), p. 136.

2. Samuel Phillips, "Mr. Thackeray's New Novel," *Times* 22 December 1852; reprinted in *The Critical Heritage,* p. 155.

3. *Thackeray* (1879); reprinted in *The Critical Heritage,* p. 166.

4. Phillips, in *The Critical Heritage,* p. 159.

5. George Brimley, "Thackeray's *Esmond,*" *Spectator,* 6 November 1852, pp. 253–62; reprinted in *The Critical Heritage,* p. 144.

6. Dudley Flamm, *Thackeray's Critics* (Chapel Hill; Univ. of North Carolina Press, 1966), p. 13.

7. Brimley, "Thackeray's *Esmond,*" p. 139.

8. Flamm, *Thackeray's Critics,* p. 12.

9. Reprinted in *The Critical Heritage,* p. 162.

10. William Makepeace Thackeray, *The History of Henry Esmond, Esq.* (New York: Holt, Rinehart and Winston, 1962), p. 487. Subsequent references will be made in the text.

11. In *Vanity Fair* and *The Newcomes* particularly, both set in his own century, Thackeray's concern with decadent forms of the medieval social order is central.

12. Juliet McMaster, *Thackeray: The Major Novels* (Toronto: Univ. of Toronto Press, 1971), p. 152, observes: "A family tree, like that of the Esmonds, Warringtons, or Newcomes, is an accumulation of relevant information about the characters who are immediately to concern us." This chapter is particularly indebted to Professor McMaster's study of Thackeray. Barbara Hardy, *The Exposure of Luxury: Radical Themes in Thackeray* (Pittsburgh:

Univ. of Pittsburgh Press, 1972), pp. 48–49, also points out Thackeray's careful use of titles as indices of his concern with genealogy: "the careful and explicit choice of titles makes it plain that this is a novel about titles, about bastardy, about claiming and essaying thrones, allegiance, fealty and legitimacy of several kinds."

13. Most of the facts of the Esmond genealogy as I discuss them in this immediate context are rather cursorily presented by Henry in an eight-page summary in chapter 2 of his autobiography (pp. 10–18).

14. Phillips, "Mr. Thackeray's New Novel," p. 157.

15. Brimley, "Thackeray's *Esmond*," p. 143.

16. We do not have only Isabella's word that she was intimate with James, though it may be impossible to prove beyond all doubt. Henry at one point refers to James II, "who, if the story was true had not always been a saint as far as she [Isabella] and many others were concerned" (p. 193). He later claims that she lost her "honour" to James (p. 487). And Beatrix Esmond also terms Isabella a "king's mistress" (p. 461).

17. McMaster, *Thackeray: The Major Novels*, p. 88: "the battle between the worldly siren and the domestic angel, with the latter apparently victorious, continued to be the basic structure of the novels [after *Vanity Fair*]." While Rachel and Isabella are opposing types in many regards, Rachel is, like Isabella, an ardent Jacobite until the end of the novel when, like Henry, she is disillusioned by the behavior of the Pretender.

18. John A. Sutherland has discussed the reasons behind Thackeray's use of footnotes to the text of Esmond's memoirs in "*Henry Esmond* and the Virtues of Carelessness," *MP* 68 (1971): 345–54.

19. John Loofbourow, *Thackeray and the Form of Fiction* (Princeton: Princeton Univ. Press, 1964), p. 131: "Beatrix assumes many masks—Dulcinea, Circe, Eve, Venus—but the motif of pseudo-Olympian chastity, inherited from the debauched old Viscountess, pursues her to the end of the novel."

20. James H. Wheatley, *Patterns in Thackeray's Fiction* (Cambridge, Mass.: MIT Press, 1969), p. 107, says of Esmond's reasons for retiring to America, "England can only hope to catch up with him."

21. Although Esmond accepts the accession of George I in favor of James III, his real choice for the next king of England seems to be his counterpart in the Stuart genealogy, the duke of Berwick: "Had Berwick been his father's heir, James the Third had assuredly sat on the English throne. He could dare, endure, strike, speak, be silent" (p. 425).

22. That Henry's account of his New World experience is probably idealized has been argued interestingly by John Hagan, "'Bankruptcy of His Heart': The Unfulfilled Life of Henry Esmond," *NCF* 27 (1972): 293–316, and J. Hillis Miller, *The Form of Victorian Fiction* (Notre Dame: Univ. of Notre Dame Press, 1968), pp. 17–25, 97–104. Barbara Hardy, *Exposure of Luxury*, p. 181, has also noted that in *Esmond*, "Love exists, and is better than 'name,' 'wealth,' and 'ambition,' but it cannot transcend them entirely." Ironic readings of Henry's narrative counter Percy Lubbock's classic account in *The Craft of Fiction* (1921; reprint, New York: Viking Press, 1957), pp. 126–41.

Chapter 5

1. William Makepeace Thackeray, *The Newcomes* (London: J. M. Dent, 1962), 2:422–23. Subsequent references will be made in the text.

2. That this is a novel whose reputation is currently undergoing review seems agreed, as Robert A. Colby has noted in *Victorian Fiction: A Second Guide to Research,* edited by George H. Ford (New York: MLA, 1978), p. 134: "We need also to see *The Newcomes* more as a representative novel of the 1850s. Meanwhile, critical revaluation of this domestic tragedy seems on the way to restoring it to the esteem it enjoyed in Thackeray's lifetime." Colby himself furthers such restoration in his *Thackeray's Canvass of Humanity: An Author and His Public* (Columbus: Ohio State Univ. Press, 1979). R. D. McMaster, "An Honorable Emulation of the Author of *The Newcomes:* James and Thackeray," *NCF* 32 (1978): 199–219, also attempts to revise the relative standing of these two major nineteenth-century authors in Thackeray's favor.

3. Edgar F. Harden, "The Artistry of a Serial Novelist: Parts 10, 14, and 15 of *The Newcomes,*" *SEL* 16 (1976): 613.

4. Jane P. Tompkins, ed., *Reader-Response Criticism: From Formalism to Post-Structuralism* (Baltimore: Johns Hopkins Univ. Press, 1980), pp. xvi–xvii.

5. For instance, see James M. Keech, "'. . . Make 'em Wait': Installment Suspense in Thackeray's *Vanity Fair,*" *Serif* 3 (1966): 9–12.

6. Juliet McMaster, *Thackeray: The Major Novels* (Toronto: Univ. of Toronto Press, 1971), p. 157, states: "The marriage market itself is of course a central image in the novel, and the repetition of the mercenary marriage and its outcome between various couples is a unifying structural principle." See also Lawrence Lerner, "Thackeray and Marriage," *Essays in Criticism* 25 (1975): 279–303.

7. Jean Sudrann, "'The Philosopher's Property': Thackeray and the Use of Time," *VS* 10 (1967): 386. Sudrann has also stressed the importance of the material in the overture in governing the structure of the entire novel (p. 379).

8. Juliet McMaster makes a parallel point: "It is part of the intricate structure of the novel that the great world which it depicts in such painstaking detail is reflected in miniature in numerous little microcosms through the book" (*Thackeray: The Major Novels,* p. 162). See also Sudrann, "'The Philosopher's Property,'" p. 379, who notes "Thackeray's familiar theme of the recurrence of all events in time."

9. Although the contention that meetings and partings are the major action of the novel is difficult to prove conclusively, a listing of the events in one chapter, along with this list from the entire novel, suggests the pervasiveness of such gatherings and dispersals: we begin chapter 49, "Six More Courses and Two Desserts," with the Pendennises' departure from a party given by Barnes Newcome, and proceed to a discussion of the guests later that night by Arthur and Laura; then we come to a party given by Clive for many of the same people; we watch Arthur and Laura's departure from there; then we see attempts by Lady Clara Pulleyn to visit or be visited by Laura Pendennis; next we witness a party at Bryanstone Square, and the Pendennises' parting from there; and last we observe a meeting of Pen and his uncle, Major Pendennis, the next day, where they contemplate giving yet another party. The narrator himself comments: "I smile as I think how much dining has already been commemorated in these veracious pages; but the story is an everyday record; and does not dining form a certain part of the pleasure and business of every day? It is at that pleasant hour that our sex has the privilege of meeting the other" (2:123). Barbara Hardy has also focused on one particular kind of meeting in chapter 5, "The Comic Feast," in her *The Exposure of Luxury: Radical Themes in Thackeray* (Pittsburgh: Univ. of Pittsburgh Press, 1972). And J. A. Sutherland has noted many scenes of parting: "what one values most in *The Newcomes* are

just such clear hard images of separation: Clive and Ethel aching for each other at the lecture on 'married bliss,' the father miserable that his son loves him best when he is absent, the Colonel on his deathbed" (*Thackeray at Work*, p. 84).

10. Jack P. Rawlins, *Thackeray's Novels: A Fiction That Is True* (Berkeley: Univ. of California Press, 1974), p. 121, notes that Thackeray "lacks a minute particularly of time and place." John Lester, "Thackeray's Narrative Technique," *PMLA* 69 (1954): 399, makes a parallel point: "Thackeray is more interested in his characters' reactions to events than he is in the events themselves."

11. McMaster, *Thackeray, The Major Novels*, p. 167.

12. W. J. Harvey, *Character and the Novel* (Ithaca: Cornell Univ. Press, 1965), p. 129, makes a fine observation about how such particularity and universality can coexist in a single work:

> in some novels we may also feel the presence of what Yeats calls tragedy (Lawrence's world of carbon); beneath the superstructure of the individualized character, we may sense those depths in which identity is submerged and united within a greater whole. And with the very greatest novels one feels that the individual character is thereby immeasurably enriched, that he is not obliterated, or dehumanized into allegory or symbol, but filled with an inexhaustible reservoir of meaning so that he becomes, as it were, a shaft of light defining the greater darkness which surrounds him. My metaphors are mixed but I trust my meaning in plain, for it points to a sense of human life, a dimension of reality, without which we should all be impoverished.

13. R. D. McMaster, "The Pygmalion Motif in *The Newcomes*," *NCF* 29 (1974): 22–39, has also touched on this essential note in Thackeray: "To the individual at the vivid center of his moment of time, his schemes seem unique and substantial. In a long view, however, he encounters the frustrations that all men encounter in a world of limitations. . . . And the contrast between the patterns the mind wishes to see fulfilled and the realities of life in the fallen world occasions Thackeray's postscript after he has . . . chopped his story short, leaving the reader's romantic longings frustrated" (p. 22).

14. Myron Taube, "Thackeray and the Reminiscential Vision," *NCF* 18 (1963): 247–59. Taube traces this "bitter-sweet backward glance" (p. 259) to events in Thackeray's life.

15. Hardy has commented on this moment: "there is an awkward and interesting middle stage [in Ethel and Clive's relationship] when Ethel and Pen [*sic*] enjoy the intimate privacy of meetings in Madame de Florac's old garden in Paris, though no actual commitments have been made, nor indeed will be made, except between the lines" (*Exposure of Luxury*, p. 174).

16. Gordon Ray, *Thackeray: The Age of Wisdom* (New York: McGraw-Hill, 1958), p. 248. Juliet McMaster, *Thackeray: The Major Novels*, pp. 163–64, has also noted the effects of serial publication on reader response to *The Newcomes*.

17. Walter Houghton, *The Victorian Frame of Mind, 1830–1870* (New Haven: Yale Univ. Press, 1957), p. 77.

18. Jerome Beaty, "All Victoria's Horses and All Victoria's Men," *NLH* 1 (1970): 290.

19. Ray, *Age of Wisdom*, p. 244: "As the end of the novel approached, Thackeray was besieged by appeals to unite his hero and heroine. . . ." Typical of original response to the ending itself might be the following comment from an unsigned review of *The Newcomes* in

the *Spectator*, 18 August 1855: "Dear old Colonel! since Lefevre died more generous tears have not been wept over a book than have fallen for you . . ." (reprinted in *Thackeray: The Critical Heritage*, edited by Geoffrey Tillotson and Donald Hawes [London: Routledge & Kegan Paul, 1968], p. 222).

20. Houghton, *Victorian Frame of Mind*, p. 85.

21. Ray, *Age of Wisdom*, p. 236, for instance, notes that Thackeray planned for two incidents in each monthly number. And more recently, Sutherland insists that "manifestly, *The Newcomes* is the only novel of which we can confidently say, 'Thackeray planned it'" (*Thackeray at Work*, p. 77).

Chapter 6

1. *Cornhill*, February 1864, p. 131.

2. *Cornhill*, February 1864, p. 136.

3. *Scribner's Magazine*, January 1901, p. 44.

4. Robert Tracy, "Instant Replay: Trollope's *The Landleaguers*, 1883," *Eire-Ireland* 15 (1980): 32.

5. *Academy*, 17 November 1883, p. 328.

6. *Spectator*, 15 December 1883, p. 1,627.

7. *Saturday Review*, 12 January 1884, p. 54.

8. *Athenaeum*, 24 November 1883, p. 666.

9. Periodicals representing the more sophisticated literary tastes were cautious in their evaluations of the fragment, but nevertheless conferred on it some artistic integrity by mentioning it at all. For example, the *Academy*, 22 October 1870, begins a tribute to Dickens with a careful admission: "Just as we are warned not to call a man's life happy till we know the manner of his death, we should withhold our final judgment on a writer till we have been enabled to compare his last work with his first, and both with his greatest" (pp. 1–2). The reviewer goes on in some detail, however, in his evaluation of *Drood*'s merits: "*The Mystery of Edwin Drood* may either be the subject of speculation as a novel, or of study as the last fragment from his fertile pen. In the first respect there are signs of a more carefully-designed intrigue than in most of his earlier works" (p. 2). The *Athenaeum*, 17 September 1870, even argues that *Drood* "is, after all, not such a fragment as it looks. In itself it is really complete. . . . [The] public will be at once sad and satisfied to take the story of 'Edwin Drood' as it is,—grateful to the author and his memory for what he achieved, and with implicit faith in him as to what he intended" (p. 362).

10. The *Illustrated London News*, 9 April 1870, sounds a familiar note among the weeklies as it looks forward to a year of reading Dickens's parts once a month: "All the world is eager to welcome Mr. Dickens back to the domains of serial fiction, and, so far as we can judge from the first number of his new work, public expectation is not likely to be disappointed" (p. 383). Three months into *Drood*'s planned twelve-month run, *Lloyd's Weekly London Newspaper*, 5 June 1870, has included the regular appearance of more of Dickens's parts in its routine: "'The Mystery of Edwin Drood' progresses admirably. Already it has become a familiar presence, and the monthly installments are waited for with no ordinary anxiety" (p. 8).

11. The *Examiner*, 18 June 1870, writing soon after Dickens's death, does not abandon the practice of reviewing new parts of *Drood* as they appear, even though it was known that

the novel would never be completed. It finds the first three numbers of *Drood* equal in quality to his other efforts: "These three numbers showed that 33 years of almost uninterrupted literary toil had not diminished either the flow of his imagination or the rigour and freshness of his diction. While regretting their abrupt curtailment, they are not an unfitting memorial of an active life" (p. 387). The *Spectator*, 11 June 1870, makes no distinction between Dickens's finished and his unfinished works in a review of his career: "But take which of his books you will, from the first to the one of which the publication had only just reached its third number at his death, and you will find the same secret of success and failure . . ." (p. 750).

12. Wolfgang Iser, *The Act of Reading: A Theory of Aesthetic Response* (Baltimore: Johns Hopkins Univ. Press, 1978), p. 114. Subsequent references will be made in the text and include page numbers in parentheses.

13. A. E. Dyson, *The Inimitable Dickens* (London: St. Martin's Press, 1970), p. 281.

14. William Makepeace Thackeray, *Denis Duval*, serialized in *Cornhill*, March–June 1864, p. 517. Subsequent references will be made in the text and include page numbers in parentheses. The novel appeared in the following pages in each month's issue: March, pp. 257–91; April, pp. 385–409; May, pp. 513–536; June, pp. 641–665.

15. Charles Dickens, *The Mystery of Edwin Drood*, ed. Stephen Holland, Stephen Lutman, and Michael Irwin (1870; facsimile reprint, Canterbury: Univ. of Kent, 1980), p. 140. Subsequent references will be made in the text and include page numbers in parentheses.

16. Roy Roussel, "The Completed Story in *The Mystery of Edwin Drood*," *Criticism* 20 (1978): 384. Subsequent references will be made in the text and include page numbers in parentheses.

17. Ina Rae Hark, "Marriage in the Symbolic Framework of *The Mystery of Edwin Drood*," *Studies in the Novel* 9 (1977): 167.

18. Earle Davis, *The Flint and the Flame: The Artistry of Charles Dickens* (Columbia: Univ. of Missouri Press, 1963), p. 156.

19. There are, of course, fewer critical analyses of these incomplete novels than of the finished works by these major authors. Furthermore, as Sylvere Monod, in *Dickens the Novelist* (Norman: Univ. of Oklahoma Press, 1968), points out of *Drood* in particular, "Unfortunately, the Drood literature is largely unconcerned with the literary merits of the book itself" (p. 490). It is not necessarily true, however, that, as Philip Collins insists in *Dickens and Crime* (London: Macmillan & Co., 1962), "no assessment of the novel . . . is possible without our making some surmise about the unwritten second half . . ." (p. 304). As Lawrence Frank suggests in "The Intelligibility of Madness in *Our Mutual Friend* and *The Mystery of Edwin Drood*," *Dickens Studies Annual* 5 (1976): 150, "All this speculation [about the mystery] obscures the integrity of the fragment as it stands." I see the effort of so many critics and enthusiasts to continue the novel as evidence of the work's force, its obvious effect on our imagination. As Andrew Sanders puts it in *Charles Dickens: Resurrectionist* (New York: St. Martin's Press, 1982), "Not completing the book, it is as if Dickens with rich symbolic intent left it all up to mankind and history" (p. 66). Paul Gottschalk, "Time in *Edwin Drood*," *Dickens Studies Annual* 1 (1970): 270, believes the story's future is "comfortably secure in the hands of its young citizens who, at the end of the novel, will be paired off to continue the natural cycle of life, death, and new life that Dickens has established at the outset." Dyson also believes that the novel "challenges us to pay attention to every detail, every notable inclusion or omission, every nuance of tone" (*The Inimitable Dickens*, p. 269).

Such analyses as Gareth Cordery's "The Cathedral as Setting and Symbol in *The Mystery of Edwin Drood*," *Dickens Studies Newsletter* 10 (1979): 97–103—which sees the Cathedral as the central symbol of the novel—and Craig Werner's "Fugal Structure in *The Mystery of the Edwin Drood*," *Dickens Studies Newsletter* 9 (1978): 77–80—which suggests that the novel proceeds in the manner of a fugue—seem to me to rest upon the assumption that only the discovery of the implied complete form of *Drood* would make it eligible for serious literary study. A central tenet of much *Drood* criticism involves the opposition between what Hillis Miller, in *Charles Dickens: The World of His Novels* (Cambridge, Mass.: Harvard Univ. Press, 1958), terms "the conventional and clarified life of a quiet English cathedral town, and the real depths below, the darkness of opium fumes, of hallucinatory visions and of the fanaticisms of the Orient . . ." (p. 320). Charles Mitchell, *"The Mystery of Edwin Drood:* the Interior and Exterior Self," *ELH* 33 (1966), is one of the few critics who does not believe that "we must finish Dickens' novel for him before we can begin to determine its significance" (p. 245). For him, the novel's "unifying agent" (p. 230) is its theme, the consequences of an opposition between the "interior" self and the "exterior" self formed in response to society. Fred Kaplan, *Dickens and Mesmerism: The Hidden Springs of Fiction* (Princeton: Princeton Univ. Press, 1975), has also discussed the theme of completeness in *Drood*, identifying Neville and Helena Landless as the "twins [in Dickens] most dedicated to the fulfillment of one another . . . two parts of a metaphor of wholeness" (p. 122) and Jasper as living in "double consciousness, with two separate states of being" (p. 154).

20. Anthony Trollope, *The Landleaguers*, with an introduction by Robert Tracy (1883; reprint, New York: Arno Press, 1981), 2:93. Subsequent references will be made in the text and include volume and page numbers in parentheses.

21. Although *The Landleaguers* was chiefly reviewed after it came out in three volumes (rather than as it appeared weekly in *Life*), some reviewers did look forward to its (unwritten) ending. The *Westminister Review*, January 1884, argues, for instance, that "though the final chapters are wanting, the *dénouement* is clearly foreshadowed" (p. 277).

22. *Examiner*, 14 May 1870, p. 311.

23. *Lloyd's Weekly London Newspaper*, 10 April 1870, p. 5.

24. *Bell's Weekly Messenger*, 2 April 1870, p. 6.

25. *News of the World*, 10 July 1870, p. 6.

26. *Academy*, 22 October 1870, p. 2. Often, too, reviewers made startlingly specific predictions, as this one from the *Graphic*, 9 April 1870: "There is evidently trouble brewing here [in regard to Rosa]. The girl will break from the condition imposed upon her, merely because it is a condition and she is of a kind who must be free, or perhaps she will marry in mere blind obedience, and afterwards repent; whence tragic incidents and bitter tears, with which it is not hard to perceive that the young husband's particular friend and relative, Jasper, the opium dreamer, will have some very close connexion" (p. 438). Some predictions are interestingly inaccurate, as is the *Weekly Dispatch's* (3 April 1870) that Rosa is "not so pretty and more stupid than little Dora [Copperfield]" (p. 6). And, of course, all predictions give credit to Dickens's ability to inspire the imagination of his readers, as *Bell's Weekly Messenger*, 4 June 1870, asserts: "Here, for example, is one of those by-strokes of power and influence which at once seize upon the reader and set him thinking, simply because of the nature which is apparent in every line" (p. 6).

27. While Forster rearranged Dickens's material (putting some of number 5 in the

unfinished, shorter number 6), the effect on the reader is still the creation of uncertainty about the future. For an explanation of the composition and publication of *Drood*'s six parts, see Margaret Cardwell's introduction to *The Mystery of Edwin Drood*, ed. Margaret Cardwell (Oxford: Clarendon Press, 1972), pp. xiii–xxxiii.

28. While the week between issues of *Life* (which contained installments of *The Land-leaguers*) allowed less time for speculation than the monthly pauses of Dickens's and Thackeray's serial formats, Trollope still leaves his reader with difficult questions at the ends of individual issues. For example, the 18 May 1883 issue (chapter 27) ends with Lord Castlewell loaning Rachel O'Mahony's father a large sum of money. Neither Rachel nor the reader is exactly sure what obligations (and rumors of obligation) this will create for her father, for herself, and for Lord Castlewell.

29. Ina Ferris, "Realism and the Discord of Endings: The Example of Thackeray," *NCF* 38 (1983): 299.

30. *Saturday Review*, 12 January 1884, p. 53. Much of the anticipation about these unfoldings of fictional worlds does involve that traditional serial element, suspense, as the *Weekly Dispatch*'s comment about *Edwin Drood* reveals: "But the reader is disposed to ask— IS JASPER GUILTY?" (10 July 1870, p. 6). Still, other responses to the ongoing story more specifically look forward to the many possibilities of development any long novel offers. The *News of the World*, 8 May 1870, sees possibilities, for instance, in the relationship of Rosa Bud and Helene Landless: "Some very exciting scenes are likely to arise from this connexion; and there is an admirable scene in the present number where the two girls are seen in striking contrast" (p. 6).

31. *Cornhill*, June 1864, p. 655.

32. *Bell's Weekly Messenger*, 2 April 1870, p. 6.

33. *Illustrated Times*, 2 April 1870, p. 218.

34. *Examiner*, 9 April 1870, p. 248.

35. *Athenaeum*, 2 April 1870, p. 443.

36. *Athenaeum*, 24 November 1883, p. 666.

37. *Guardian*, 10 April 1864, p. 338.

38. *Press*, 4 June 1864, p. 548.

39. *Spectator*, 11 June 1870, p. 750.

40. *Spectator*, 11 June 1870, p. 750. The *Examiner*, 10 September 1870, further claims that Dickens's creative powers never waned in his career: "To the last stroke of the pen, indeed, the glorious imagination seems not to have faltered or faded, and those who would expect to find some indication of waning power in this his last chapter may find their ideas falsified in the following lines . . ." (p. 583). Equally admiring of Dickens's inexhaustible ability to create is the *Academy*, 22 October 1870: ". . . Dickens is to the Briton what a story from the *Arabian Nights* is to the Oriental; it is the invention of a single man against the memory of a generation of grandmothers" (p. 3). The *Graphic*, 17 September 1870, makes the same point about Trollope: "Wonderful man this Mr. Trollope! One fancies he could sit down spinning out fictitious love letters in Sedan with the Prussian shells bursting over his head" (p. 275).

The pressures serialization placed upon the creativity of Victorian authors—not only to meet deadlines but also to continue to satisfy audiences—are well known. See, for example, the account of Thackeray's difficulties provided by Sutherland (*Thackeray at Work*, pp. 111–

12). However, we also need to recall how the serial novelist's close contact with actual readers often inspired authors, as noted by Kathleen Tillotson in *Novels of the Eighteen-Forties* (London: Oxford Univ. Press, 1954), pp. 33–39, and Sutherland, p. 127.

41. Jerome Beaty, "All Victoria's Horses and All Victoria's Men," *NLH* 1 (1970): 291–92.

42. *Examiner,* 18 June 1870, p. 387.

43. *Weekly Times,* 4 September 1870, p. 2.

44. *Illustrated Times,* 8 October 1870, p. 231.

Index

Michael Lund received his M.A. and Ph.D. from Emory University. An associate professor of English at Longwood College, Dr. Lund has published a number of articles on Victorian fiction.

The manuscript was edited by Christina Postema. The book was designed by Joanne Elkin Kinney. The typeface for the text is Galliard. The display types are Albertus and Galliard. The book is printed on 55–lb. Glatfelter text paper and is bound in Holliston Mills' Roxite Linen.

Manufactured in the United States of America.